THE

Metamorphosis

THE Metamorphosis

A DYMOND STORY

Sherri Sanjurjo

CONCLUSIO
HOUSE PUBLISHING

"The Metamorphosis"
Printed in Canada
First Printing, 2015

ISBN: 978-0-9949204-1-6

Published by:

Conclusio House Publishing
503-7700 Hurontario Street
Suite 209
Brampton, ON
L6Y 4M3

www.conclusiohouse.com

Disclaimer: *Except for those who have given their expressed permission, all names and identifiable characteristics have been changed to protect the true identities of individuals mentioned in this book.*

I dedicate this book to my children. This book is proof that there is nothing impossible with God. When change comes into your life to break you, morph and let the Lord shape you into His image. Momma loves you.

Acknowledgment

I have to acknowledge my Father, who created me for His glory and raised me when my parents weren't able to. He pursued me while I stumbled in the darkness and loved me back to life. My life is yours, Lord, have your way.

I would be crazy if I didn't acknowledge two very dear people in my life, who encouraged me and pushed me when I felt like this just wasn't going to happen—Michelle Cwihun and Barbara Brown. Michelle, thank you for spending so much time with me on this book and allowing me to see the book through your eyes. I love you dearly. "B", a.k.a. Mamita, you are my sister for life. I honestly thank God for you on the regular. Your kick in the butt at times reminded me of the importance of this project. We are not just friends, you are my sister.

To *Conclusio House Publishing*, thank you so much, Kerri-Ann Haye-Donawa, for hearing my story and coming along for this portion of the journey. You are a priceless gem.

Lastly, to all my Dymond Girls, you know who you are. I have to acknowledge how you have changed my life drastically. Thank you for allowing me to see life through your eyes. Thank you for the testimonies that keep me doing what I feel I've been created to do for you. Remember, when life changes in a way you weren't expecting, it's an opportunity for you to transform into your most authentic self.

Thank you all for the love and support.

Table of Contents

Preface

I don't consider myself anyone special, and I'm certainly not innocent by any means. I've done dirt and made my share of mistakes that have taught me real life lessons that, today, I'm grateful for. But if there is one thing I do know about myself, it is this: I am real, and I am passionate. I'm as passionate as Martin Luther King Jr. was on August 28, 1963. I am passionate about empowering people to experience their own authenticity and find their reason to hope again, dream again, believe again.

We've lost the ability to hope for a life that can be fulfilling and joyful, even in the midst of chaos and tragedy. We think dreaming is for the birds, and hope is something that very few of us experience regularly, even though deep down we all really want to. Well, I'm a dreamer, y'all! I am a self-confessed, absolutely incurable, ridiculous, the-bigger-the-better, anything-can-happen dreamer. Even though my dreams have been changed and damaged by life's unexpected pitfalls and bad choices, I somehow stayed connected to my dreams. Dreams keep hope alive. My dreams kept me alive.

Here's the thing about dreams, they can change in a blink of an eye. A death, a divorce, a birth, losing your job, losing your self confidence, the list can go on and on, and in a moment your dreams can change, and so can your life. Now change, it's inevitable and beautiful and painful and hard and amazing because it gives us the opportunity to grow into our most authentic selves and experience something that we never have before. What throws us off key sometimes is the fact that change can hurt like an open vein on an ice cube, even when it's for the best. I've learned through some hard life lessons that when I embrace change and transform with it, instead of fight it, I become the best version of myself, and I get to live on purpose. I experience a joy that I don't have words to aptly describe, but it's real. I want that for you, too.

So here I am, literally an open book for you to read. It's an inside look into my childhood and teenage years. A close look into a life that wasn't supposed to be here, a life that was full of brokenness, abuse, wounds, and rejection. It's about a life that wasn't supposed to mean much or accomplish anything important, a life where shattered dreams were repaired because I learned the beauty of morphing and transforming like a caterpillar into a butterfly.

Now, let me be clear about the integrity of this book, and I say this mindful of Sister Souljah's book, *No Disrespect* (my cherished literary inspiration). This is a work of non-fiction. All the stories are based on the reality of my life. The conversations held years ago are freely recreated. Their essence is as true as my memory would permit me to share. The names as well as certain details have been changed to protect the innocent and the guilty and to avoid embarrassing anyone other than myself. The important thing is not who these people are but the circumstances that each person had to deal with in order to survive or thrive. The stories are experiences that happened in my life or in the life of others who were, or are, connected to me in some way. I've purposely changed the names to protect them and by no means intend to be disrespectful. However, I am unapologetic about the truth, because I believe that when the truth is exposed it has the power to set you free. Yes, even when the truth hurts.

Truth brings change, but change is hard and, sometimes, not easily welcomed. Shoot, sometimes change is purposely rejected because it feels like the pain of truth outweighs the blessing and benefits that truth brings with it. But I don't want you to be tricked to believe that lie. Lies tear down and destroy. Truth rebuilds and restores.

This is my truth.

On May 13, 1970, I was birthed into this world as Sherri D. Sanjurjo, but when shattered dreams, broken promises, and the pain that took my breath away were finished, I was reborn as Dymond.

When dreams change without warning, you are automatically, and sometimes unwillingly, thrown into *The Metamorphosis*. I pray my story will show you how to embrace your own personal metamorphosis when it comes; and if it hasn't yet, then brace yourself because it will. I pray that you, too, will experience the wonderful abundance of life that hope can bring in the midst of overwhelming tragedy.

Wishing you a wonderful *process*,

Sherri Sanjurjo
(a.k.a. Dymond)

Part 1

"LAY THE EGG AND BOUNCE"

Reality Check

*"Love is hard to recognize at times, but is seen
most clearly when pain has washed your eyes."*
~Dymond

Jocelyn woke up on the floor in a pool of blood. She had collapsed in the blood after vomiting for hours over a toilet bowl she wished she had cleaned the week before. Her head felt like someone had hit her with a brick at least twice, and she couldn't see clearly. Everything was blurry, and she was confused.

How did she get here?

She tried to pull herself up slowly, trying to remember what happened, but the room just wouldn't stop spinning. She didn't know if it was her head or the smell of the toilet that was causing the dizziness. She tried to push away the fumes with her hand as if she were shooing a fly, but it wasn't working. It seemed like the more alert she became the stronger the smell became also. The last thing she remembered was having an argument with Devon. "Lord, what am I gonna do now?" she whispered to herself,

Jocelyn had never seen him that angry before and didn't know if she would ever see him again. She thought telling him the good news would draw them closer together, but instead it drove him into an uncontrollable rage. She wondered if she would ever hear his sexy Nuyorican accent again, feel his tender touch, or ever be in his arms again. Those arms used to bring her a sense of safety, but now she knew his arms to do other things, like shake the hell out of her, push her away, and throw her to the ground. She took a deep breath and slowly pulled herself up off the cold, black-and-white checkered, tiled floor.

Only apartments in the Bronx have these ugly, cold ass floors.

She felt a sharp pain in her stomach, "Ouch!" She used her left hand to slowly push herself up, her right hand automatically rubbing her stomach where it hurt, as if the rubbing would somehow stop the pain. Then it all came back to her. She was twelve weeks pregnant with his baby, and he wanted nothing to do with her or "it." She already had a three-year-old son, what the hell was she going to do with another baby and no father to help her or, more importantly, love her?

She used the bathtub to steady herself and get her to the sink. When she got to the sink and looked in the mirror, she was horrified. The left side of her face was covered in blood and vomit, her lip was swollen and busted, and there was blood on her teeth, too. She turned on the water and started washing it off frantically, and then stopped. The tears came without warning like an uncontrollable river. Her face turned red immediately, and she just let it out. The sink was still holding her up, and the pain was still in her stomach, but it was honestly the last thing she was thinking about. As she looked at herself in the mirror, not recognizing who was staring back at her, she asked herself in the most annoyed voice she could muster, "How the hell did I get here? How did I let this happen?"

Her thoughts were foggy as she tried to remember how she had reached this new rock bottom. Just then, gospel music came blaring through the bathroom window, and she remembered…it all started in church.

About six months ago, Jocelyn's closest friend, Antoinette, invited her to a church in Harlem. She invited her almost every week, but Jocelyn would always make excuses so she wouldn't hurt her feelings.

"Nah, girl, I'm mad busy. But hit me up around Easter, okay?" What she really wanted to say was, *"Hell nah, I ain't going to no church with all those hypo-Christians. Is you crazy?"* But she didn't. She cared about Antoinette way too much to be honest.

Anoinette was the only real friend she had. So she kept making excuses, dodging church every time she was asked. Except for the time when Jocelyn had to admit, even to herself, that she was at one of her lowest moments in life. She knew she needed help getting her life together 'cause it was a mess and out of control. There was too much alcohol and drugs in her life. She was sleeping with random men for money and, sometimes, love and acceptance. It was a confusing time in her life. Without even realizing it, sleeping with strangers evolved into how she paid the bills and made her feel some sort of importance.

When Antoinette had asked her to go to church, like she normally did, she agreed because she felt like she was hitting rock bottom and this may be her only chance. Jocelyn was looking for a satisfaction that wasn't being fulfilled by alcohol, drugs, or strange men. She'd never hit rock bottom before, and it scared the crap out of her. Deciding to go to church at this point was a decision made out of pure desperation.

Maybe if I go to church I might find a way to make better choices...do things differently...have more hope for my future, she thought. *Something's gotta change. I don't know if this will work, but I need to do something, 'cause what I'm doing right now ain't working.*

Jocelyn thought maybe she'd be able to meet new people who would really care about her, and then she would drop the 'frienemies' that surrounded her all the time. She finally gave in and said to herself, *What have I got to lose? I used to know God real good back in the day until I met 'the Reverent.'*

The 'Reverent' was Jocelyn's ex-husband. He was a pastor who was cheating on her throughout their marriage with women in the church. To her they had the perfect marriage, but in truth it was the perfect lie. He was a professional conman from the Caribbean that was looking for someone to help him get to the U.S., and she was the last to know. As far as she knew, he was a man of God. Wasn't it okay to trust him? The marriage lasted seven years, and then one day she came home to their apartment and it was empty. He had taken everything. Everything! He left her clothes but took every stick of furniture with him. He ran up her credit cards and left her with the debt and heartache. He had received his Permanent Resident Card the week before and no longer needed her, so he bounced. It took years for

Jocelyn to get out of debt. She was left to rebuild her life alone and didn't know what she had done so wrong to deserve that kind of treatment.

After that experience, she met the father of her son in a nightclub. Still looking for love, Jocelyn was caught up in a whirlwind romance. Michael treated her like gold. He cared about her so much. No man had ever been so protective and caring before. She was in love and before she knew it, she was pregnant with his baby. Everything was wonderful. He was attentive, kind, loving, and as fine as a man could be.

One day, they were heading to an event on the bus, and he noticed another man staring at her. Jocelyn hadn't even acknowledged the man staring at her, but Michael was convinced they were having an affair. He started yelling and calling her all kinds of disrespectful names. Jocelyn was in shock and tried to calm him down. *Why was he acting like this? And why would he think this?* It was crazy!

"You bitch! You gonna sit here next to me with your man right there?" he shouted. "Is you crazy? You're nothing but a nasty, dirty slut. I don't know what I saw in your ass. You disgust me!"

Jocelyn was confused and scared. She'd never seen him act like this before and didn't understand what he was talking about. His face even looked different; it was all twisted and mean. She just wanted to get off the bus. She felt so humiliated.

"I ain't stupid! I ain't blind! I see y'all lookin' at each other like I'm not even here." Michael continued in a crazy rant. "But I got your number, you nasty good for nothing whore. You're nothing but an easy lay anyway. Ain't worth shit!"

Just then, he stood up and slapped her across the

face so hard she screamed. She was so afraid of what was going to happen next that she ran off the bus before he could lay another hand on her. Jocelyn ran the rest of the way home without looking back. If she did look back she would have seen her once loving boyfriend beating on an innocent man. What Jocelyn didn't know then was that he was on medication for paranoid schizophrenia, and that day he decided he was cured and didn't need to take his pills anymore. She stopped seeing him and stopped taking his calls, but he sent a message through one of her girlfriends one day asking if he could come over to apologize. She was pregnant with her first child, living in New York City alone, and she was really hoping that the incident was just a one off. But she was still very afraid. After going back and forth in her mind with the different possible scenarios, Jocelyn agreed to see him one last time but wouldn't let him into her apartment. She decided to meet him downstairs at the front door of her building. She stood there refusing to come out onto the sidewalk to talk to him, not trusting what he might do. They stared at each other in awkward silence for a full minute.

"Okay, I'm here," Jocelyn said abruptly. "So whatchu gotta say to me?"

"I'm so sorry, Jocelyn, I had some medication that I was supposed to take that morning, but I felt so good without it that I decided not to take it. I've been diagnosed with something called paranoid schizophrenia, but I don't think that's the real problem."

Jocelyn was shocked and felt so stupid. How could she be in a relationship with a man and not know he had a serious mental illness? She felt like a fool and immediately felt compassion for him. It wasn't his fault that he acted crazy, it was because he hadn't taken his meds. He really wasn't like that. She still didn't feel safe enough to be in a relationship with him, but she did feel sorry for him.

"I'll understand if you never want to see me again, but you're having our baby, and I would like to keep in touch to be there for him or her." He asked if he could get one last kiss.

She thought of all the good times they had shared and the tender way he had been with her and decided to trust him one last time. After all, he sounded rational, and it was just to say goodbye.

As she stepped out to give him something to remember her by, something happened that she would never have expected in a million years. This crazy-ass negro punched her in her six-month-pregnant belly and said, "I hope you and that baby both die and go to hell." He then turned and walked away.

Jocelyn fell to her knees, gasping for her next breath. She was sure her baby was dead. It was at least five minutes before she could get her breath, pull herself up from the ground, and stagger back into her apartment. She kept checking her underwear for blood. Nothing. It was nothing short of a miracle that less than an hour later she felt the baby moving and kicking up a storm.

Why did she even think to trust him, much less have compassion for him? "Never again," she whispered to herself as she rubbed her very round belly.

Jocelyn said a quiet prayer for her unborn child and prayed for strength for herself. She kept on watching for signs of a miscarriage, but the pregnancy continued as scheduled, and three months later Julian was born. A beautiful baby boy. But Jocelyn was still alone, and now bitter and depressed. Even though her choice of men sucked, she still felt like maybe one day she would find true love.

When Antoinette invited her to church this time, she thought, "Why not? It can't get any worse."

When it came to church, she painted every minister, preacher, pastor, church-goer, and Christian with the same brush. *They're all crazy liars who just use people and take their money! They're all hypocrites!*

She knew it wasn't fair to judge all of them like that, but her pain spoke louder than ration and reason. She kept her inner thoughts to herself and went to church anyway, secretly hoping someone would prove her wrong. She was thankful she could find a babysitter for Julian because he wouldn't be able to sit through a church service.

Jocelyn could already hear the music as she walked toward the doors of the church. It was loud, and the beat was bumpin', whether she knew the song or not didn't matter. Anyone listening to that life-giving music was compelled to clap and move to the beat, whether they had rhythm or not.

The usher was a full-figured black lady with a beautiful white smile. Her black hair was swept over the left part of her forehead and carefully, yet very tightly, brushed up into a bun. She had white gloves on and handed Jocelyn a small comic book tract that was entitled *This Was Your Life*. Jocelyn walked in as the choir was singing, *"I'm going up yondah...going up yondah ahh, going up yondah ahh to be with my Lord!"*

Singing was something Jocelyn loved to do when she wanted to feel some sort of peace, but her heart was far from that feeling and had been for a while. She decided to take a seat and just listen to the choir. The usher tried to lead her to a seat close to the front of the church, but Jocelyn wasn't trying to be too close to the preacher man. Jocelyn pointed to a seat closer to the back of the church and looked to the usher to make sure it was cool. Usher Patsy nodded that it was fine, so Jocelyn proceeded to the seat. She said "Excuse me" a few times as she maneuvered her way past the people in her aisle, trying hard to not step on anyone's feet.

"Let's see what this preacher man has to say," she mumbled under her breath.

She hadn't spoken to God in years. *Will He even want to talk to me after everything I've done?* she wondered.

Jocelyn settled into her seat and looked around quickly for her friend, Antoinette, who was sitting closer to the front of the church. Antoinette was fully engaged in all the singing, clapping, and dancing that seemed to be commonplace at this church. They started to slow down the pace of the song, and then right in the middle they changed it up to a completely different song. This one was a familiar song, so she decided to close her eyes and quietly sing.

"I don't know why Jesus loves me, I don't know why He cares, I don't know why He sacrificed His life, oh but I'm glad, I'm glad He did."

Mmm hmm, she loved her some Andraé Crouch. It was like he just knew how she felt and sang all the words that were in her heart.

Soul Saving Station for Every Nation was a church where pushers, pimps, prostitutes, and people from all walks of life were given hope to believe that no matter what they did or were doing,

"God will love you just the way you are."

"He died just for you, and no matter what has happened in your life, He still has good plans for you. So don't you dare give up!" the preacher yelled.

Jocelyn had become an alcoholic and a prostitute and didn't know how she got to this point in her life but felt like a hot mess. She was in desperate need of hope, something she had lost long ago. While singing with her eyes shut, she felt her right hand sneak out from her lap and stretch high into the air. She felt an unspeakable drawing that was compelling her to reach past her feelings and praise God. Even though she wasn't sure how to act, her hand knew how to respond to this extraordinary presence and was already a witness to the entire experience. After the song was finished, she opened her eyes. She felt maybe…just maybe…God could love her, again.

The pastor preached about the prodigal son, and Jocelyn felt like he was talking directly to her. *Did somebody talk to this man about me? Maybe Antoinette told him my business, and that's why everything he's saying is punching me in the face right now.*

By the time he got to the end of his sermon, his shirt was soaking wet with sweat. He was breathing heavy and looked exhausted, but it was like something in him was giving him some kind of extra strength. He kept going, talking about the unconditional love of God.

"God wants you to come home so you can experience His love." It looked like he was looking for somebody in the audience, then he randomly asked, "Is there anyone here who wants to know this love personally? Come, I want to pray for you. If you want Jesus to live in your heart, come. If you need His help, come. He's waiting for you."

Jocelyn knew this was the thing she needed to get her life back on track, but she wasn't the only one there that needed that very same thing. Before she knew it, her whole face was wet from the tears that washed her high caramel cheekbones. She was overwhelmed with the feeling that there was love in the room, waiting for her to respond.

She couldn't wait any longer. Her feet started to move, even though she was still internally battling with the decision. She barely glanced at the person next to her as she said, "Excuse me. Excuse me, please." She pushed her way past the people in her row to head down to the front of the church for prayer. She started to walk quickly, then found herself running to the altar, crying uncontrollably as the choir sang, *"I surrender all, I surrender all, all to thee my precious Savior."*

Jocelyn needed a Saviour. She felt warm in her chest area and, for the first time in a long time, hope was creeping back into her life, again. She surrendered her heart to the Lord and, even though she didn't understand how it happened, she felt brand new. The preacher man was going from person to person praying for everyone. Jocelyn was so overwhelmed with the thought of Jesus loving her still after all she had done that she hadn't noticed she was next in line for prayer. The pastor came to her and said, "Do you want to be saved?"

"Yes," she answered before he could finish the sentence.

The pastor asked for one of his prayer warriors—one of the mothers of the church—to embrace her as he prayed for her. Wow, he was so respectful to her as a woman. Jocelyn felt a bit awkward but was grateful he was so willing to spend the time to pray for her. He had an entourage of people with him, just in case people fell to the ground or needed one-on-one ministry. This beautiful lady, who was already praying, embraced Jocelyn with both arms.

"Repeat after me," the pastor instructed, "Lord Jesus, please forgive me, I'm a sinner."

"Lord Jesus, please forgive me, I'm a sinner," Jocelyn repeated.

"I believe you are the Son of God, and you died to save me from sin."

"I believe you are the Son of God, and you died to save me from sin."

"Wash me and make me clean with your precious blood, and make me your daughter."

"Wash me and make me clean with your precious blood, and make me your daughter."

"In Jesus's name. Amen."

"In Jesus's name. Amen." Jocelyn repeated everything, word for word.

"Welcome to the family of God, Sis. It's good to have you back home." The lady holding her and praying with the pastor whispered in her ear. "We're here for you anytime you need us. Call me anytime. My name is Sister Patricia." The pastor went on to pray for someone else, but Jocelyn was just so grateful for the love that was poured out on her at that altar. She just knew her life was going to be different now.

She left the altar, still wiping her face with the tissue someone must have put in her hand while she was being prayed for, and headed back to her seat where Antoinette was waiting for her.

Antoinette couldn't wait to grab Jocelyn. She was jumping and hugging her, saying, "I'm so happy for you, girl!" She knew of Jocelyn's constant struggle with low self-esteem and alcohol, and how the combination of those two things put her in a bad place. "Girl, I'm so proud of you! You made the best decision you could ever make, but it's not gonna be easy." She hugged her tightly.

Jocelyn sighed, "Yeah, I know, right? For real, Ann, I really believe I can make it this time, but I'm really gonna need you, girl. I ain't strong like you."

"Girl, please, you know I gotchu. You're gonna be fine. I gotta go, girl, my kids are hungry. You okay to get home by yourself?"

Jocelyn wasn't sure, but she smiled and said,

"Yeah, I'll be fine. Go, go, go, I'll call you later." Jocelyn sat there for a while trying to calm down from the whirlwind of emotions she had just experienced. That brand new feeling started to wear off when she thought, *How am I gonna resist the temptation to drink?* She thought about how she was going to get through that night, and then she saw him.

He was walking through the crowd of people, and it looked like he was coming straight towards her. He was fine and smooth. Looked like he could have been on the cover of some classy men's magazine.

Wow...celebrities come to this church?

His walk was a confident saunter as he approached her. She was impressed by how well he was dressed. Brother looked like he was heading to a photo shoot, for real. His skin was a smooth caramel complexion. His hair was black as the night, and he wore it slicked back so you could see his chiseled features, sexy bedroom eyes, and get lost in the waves of his hair.

He wore a white linen suit, and she could tell it was custom made because it fit him perfectly. He had a couple of buttons unbuttoned at the top of his shirt that revealed a little of his chest. It wasn't hard to tell he worked out very regularly. He smelled good, too. The closer he got the more distinct the cologne became. She felt a little uncomfortable because it looked like he was coming right for her. She wanted to look somewhere else but was so impressed with him she couldn't take her eyes off him.

Devon had already made an impression on her without saying a word. "Are you okay?" he asked.

"I saw you crying at the altar."

His Puerto Rican accent was so exotic and sexy that it was hard for her to concentrate on what he actually said. After a few moments she realized he had asked her a question, and she had yet to answer him. She felt kind of embarrassed about him noticing her at the altar crying. She didn't know anyone was watching her, but he was smiling at her with a look of sincerity and understanding so she ignored the hot redness that rushed to her cheeks. "Yeah, I'm okay," she responded, "I've just been through a lot, and I've been holding it in for a long time. I guess I just needed to let it out."

He asked if he could sit down beside her. She nodded and quickly moved over in the pew so there was more room.

He continued to talk, "I know how you feel, mami. I've been battling some things myself, and I gave my heart to the Lord today because I need help seriously, you know? Oh, by the way, my name is Devon."

She knew better than anybody how he felt. She thought maybe he might be able to understand what she was going through, but her thoughts were interrupted because all she could think of was how fine he was.

They talked for what seemed to be hours, even though it was just a few moments. She felt like she knew him forever. At the end of the conversation, he asked if he could make sure she got home safely by driving her home.

Damn fine and a car? Oh Lord!

She wasn't used to that kind of treatment from a man, and although she longed to be treated with some sort of importance, she really didn't know how to act when it was offered.

"Um, yeah, sure, why not?" She was a working girl, who knew how to handle herself in the street, but he was being real nice and, although that was strange for her, she found herself wanting to stay in his presence. They walked outside together, and as they approached a beautiful car, Jocelyn thought, *There's no way this is his car.* He walked right up to it, opened the door with the key, and invited her into the front passenger's seat.

Devon drove a black BMW. It didn't matter what year or what series it was, it was beautiful. Grey leather seats and immaculately clean with the smell of lemon in the air. Jocelyn kept it hidden, but she was very impressed.

Devon did most of the talking. Jocelyn wanted to hear everything so she could find out what type of man he was. He talked all the way to her house about how he felt the pastor was speaking directly to him and what his life was like. Jocelyn was happy to hear that someone else felt the same as she did.

"Me too! Wow, I thought I was the only one!" she jumped in the middle of his sentence.

They pulled up in front of Jocelyn's building. Devon parked and said, "Let me walk you to your door. I'm glad I got you home safe. This part of the Bronx is kinda rough. Listen, thank you for listening to me babble on, mami, you're a good listener. I think you and me are a little bit the same, no?"

"You weren't babbling, you were talking and, honestly, I appreciate you talking to me so openly. I thought I was the only person with issues, but I can see we're all going through something. Anyway, it's nice to know I'm not crazy."

As they both walked to her apartment, Jocelyn caught him looking at her booty a few times. She smiled, knowing she could have more than a conversation with him if she wanted. She felt it coming—he was about to invite himself in, and she had already decided that she was gonna give him some, even if he didn't have enough money.

They got to her door and he said, "Well, have a good night...um...maybe I'll see you in church again next week."

What? He ain't gonna try to make a move? Is he blind? Maybe he's gay; his car was immaculate. Well, she was about to find out one way or another.

"Thank you so much for bringing me home, Devon. I usually don't take rides with men I don't know," she lied. "You're a real gentleman. I actually understand you more than you think, so thanks for talkin' to me." Jocelyn knew exactly what to do. She had done it a hundred times, and right now Devon looked like he was more than ready to handle what she was about to put on him.

She leaned in to give a goodnight hug, and before she knew it, he placed his right hand around her waist gently and pulled her close. And then ever so gently, he kissed her. The kiss was endearing, and after they had shared such intimate details with each other she felt like he deserved it (she would tell herself anything to justify it).

She was drawn into his gentle touch, and it didn't hurt that he was so damn fine. As she pulled out of the embrace, he whispered, "You're real special, J," and gently kissed her lips, again. This time ever so slightly, just enough for her to respond, and she did. His lips were soft, and his embrace became stronger. The kiss went from *goodbye* to *hello*. She felt it through his pants.

Boom! Got him.

They kissed for what seemed like at least five minutes, but it really was just a few seconds. Jocelyn pulled away so it wouldn't look like she was as desperate as she was.

Devon caught himself, "I'm so sorry, I'm so very sorry. I don't know what happened just now, I couldn't resist. I feel a strong drawing to you, Jocelyn, that I'm not sure how to explain. Please forgive me if I'm being too froward."

Jocelyn turned her back to him after giving him a sweet smile. Then she went into her purse and got her keys.

Jocelyn looked at him as she opened her apartment door, and almost with a whisper said, "No need to apologize. I know how you feel, I feel the same way." She took his hand and drew him into her apartment. Julian was at the babysitter's for the night, and they would be all alone. It was about to be on!

At that moment, Jocelyn decided that she would be there for him and maybe in turn he would love her. She was an alcoholic and an ex-prostitute. He was a fine Puerto Rican man who just gave his heart to God. He must be a good person. Besides, they were on the same path, trying to better their lives. She didn't know much about who he was, but she knew she wanted him, and she was gonna give him something that would make him crave her.

They were two broken, wounded souls in need of love, and she felt she had enough to give him. Not much for herself, but for him she had all the love in the world. She stepped into her one bedroom apartment that definitely needed some attention. Devon locked the door behind them, and the rest was history. They became inseparable.

They went everywhere together. He was going to help her change her life so she could put the alcohol and prostitution behind her for good.

There was only one problem.

Jocelyn didn't know that no amount of love, passion, good sex, or hope was going to be able to free Devon from his own demons. But she was about to find out. The hard way.

It Hurt

"Your past mistakes don't condemn you, they just show me where you've been while looking for Him." ~Dymond

Jocelyn stared at herself in the mirror and painfully remembered everything that happened. How she got in the state that she was in, what she did, and the damage that had been done. She remembered out loud and cried bitterly, "Oh God, I loved Devon so much I couldn't see the truth. I couldn't see who he was, and now I'm pregnant again. Oh God…Jesus, please help me. I didn't mean to do this." She looked down and touched her stomach. Her slender, petite frame was already beginning to change shape. She immediately felt a horrified guilt and whispered, "I'm sorry, little one, your mama's a mess."

Devon's words echoed through her mind like someone was yelling it in the Grand Canyon, "Abort it or it's over, over, over, over!"

That was the only way he would stay and the only way she might have a chance of having a family or love. She thought he would have been happy about the baby. But instead of tears of joy, she was now shedding tears of horrific pain, emotionally and physically. She felt like she was going to throw up again but didn't have time to get to the toilet this time, so it ended up in the tub. She was vomiting blood now. There was nothing else in her stomach... except what was left of a baby.

Jocelyn knew she had to get to the doctor to see exactly what damage she had actually done. She washed her face again, rinsed out her mouth, took a few deep breaths. She brushed back her hair, trying to look somewhat normal. She saw the clothes she had on last night on the floor outside the door. How could she not realize that she was standing in her bra and panties? It was like all of her senses were off, but she knew what she had to do. She had to try to right this wrong.

Even though she felt like a mess, she didn't want to go outside looking like one. Her clothes always complimented her figure and spoke for her. Jocelyn had a style that said sophistication, elegance, and class. She didn't fit in at all in the South Bronx or this life, but this was her life, her very hard bed; she made it, and now she was going to have to sleep in it. She staggered into the bedroom to get some fresh clothes, still rubbing her belly. After she finished putting on her clothes she looked for her handbag and found it on the kitchen table with no wallet. *Damn you, Devon!* He had taken the last bit of cash she had. She was going to use that for a taxi to go to the doctor's office. She looked around to see if there was any cash lying around, but after heading towards the bedroom she noticed all of Devon's clothes were gone. Some of the drawers were left open and were empty, and the closet door was open, and hangers were there instead of his suits. His shoes, his jewelry…all gone. He was gone, and if he was gone then every last dollar that was ever in this apartment was gone with him. Jocelyn sat at the edge of the bed in despair and started to sob uncontrollably.

"What am I supposed to do now? Oh God, please help me….I didn't mean to do this."

A sharp pain gripped her stomach and took her breath away. It lasted for about ten seconds, and she knew she had to get to the doctor right away. She slowly got up, got her balance, then started to walk towards the bedroom door, holding on to the wall. She made a left into the kitchen, reached for one of the chairs, passed the table, and got to the door. Jocelyn felt like the whole world was spinning but knew she had to try to get to the doctor or she might die. She unlocked all the locks on the front door. When she got to the third lock she was more than annoyed.

"Why are there so many damn locks on this door?"

She finally got the door opened and walked three steps across the hall to her next door neighbour, Rafael. She used all of the strength she had left to bang on his door.

"Rafael! Rafael, please open the door if you're there! Please be there…Rafael!" She banged and screamed before the door opened. Rafael had been sleeping. After all, it was six o'clock in the morning, and he worked late.

"Que te pasa, mamita? What's wrong….what happeneen to you, mami?"

"Oh, thank God you're here. I'll explain later, I just need to get to the doctor's office right now. Oww!" Another sharp pain hit her and she doubled over in the building hallway.

Rafael caught her as she was going down. "Okay, okay, I gotchu, mami, don't worry, but are you okay? What the hell's goin on, mami? Nevermind, tell me on the way. Let me just put some clothes on, and I'll take you to the doctor's, okay? Come in and sientate aqui, mamita."

Rafael was Puerto Rican, and one of her regulars. He hadn't seen her in a while because she had been with Devon, but he knew it was just a matter of time before they broke up and she would be back to him. Regardless, she was in need of help, and she knew Rafael had a good heart. He would make sure she was okay.

Rafael got dressed in seconds. Jocelyn was still holding her stomach and moaning, rocking back and forth and speaking to herself. It sounded like she was praying, but he wasn't sure.

"Okay, mami, let's go." He carefully lifted her from the bed and slowly walked her to the door. After propping her on the wall, he locked his door then turned and asked her where her jacket was.

She handed him her keys. "On the chair in the kitchen."

Rafael quickly opened the door—they had the same amount of locks on their doors—grabbed her jacket and handbag, and ran back to Jocelyn. She was still talking to herself and rubbing her stomach. He got her in the car and put her seatbelt on, ran to the other side, and headed toward Bronx Lebanon Hospital.

"I know you wanna go to the doctor, but I'm taking you to the hospital, mi amor. You don't look so good an' I don't think the doctor can help whatchu got goin on."

"Okay, okay, just get there."

Rafael drove as fast as he could, and they got to the hospital in record time. Trying to find a parking spot in the Bronx was like trying to find a police officer in the hood, they're everywhere but you can never find the one you want when you really need one.

Rafael finally found a parking spot close to the emergency door and ran to the other side of the car to help Jocelyn out. She was spitting blood, moaning, and rubbing her stomach. He gently lifted her out of the car and threw her arm around his neck. Jocelyn was extremely weak and had lost most of the colour in her face. They walked into the emergency and saw all kinds of people with all kinds of reasons to be there, but Rafael was focused on getting Jocelyn some help. They both stood at a desk where a nurse was obviously overwhelmed and overworked, looking pissed off. Rafael didn't care what or who she was mad at, so he spoke loudly enough for her to hear the urgency in his voice.

"Excuse me…nurse…excuse me…por favor, we need some help here. My friend is really sick. I think someone did something to her."

The nurse turned to Jocelyn and asked very gently, "What's wrong, sweetie?"

"I'm twelve weeks pregnant, and a few hours ago I drank turpentine, whiskey, and something else I can't remember the name of, in hopes of aborting this baby." She coughed almost on cue and couldn't stop. It felt like her stomach was betraying her, and she really couldn't blame it if it was. She was hunched over, gripping her stomach with a vengeance, hoping that she wasn't too late and feeling ashamed of her actions.

Rafael was holding her up the whole time but couldn't believe what he just heard Jocelyn say. "We need a wheelchair or sunthing!" He panicked.

The nurse looked at Jocelyn square in the eye after she stopped coughing and then looked at another nurse and said, "Let's get her a bracelet, and call the doctor right away."

Rafael ran and got a wheelchair for her to sit in.

The nurse kept calm and continued to ask the normal intake questions—full name, address, name of doctor, any allergies—and printed out some papers that would later tell the doctor everything he needed to know about the situation. After printing all of the necessary paperwork, the nurse looked at Jocelyn with gentle, caring eyes and asked, "Now why would you do that to yourself, sweetie?"

Jocelyn looked down, feeling ashamed and embarrassed. "I…I was…I…was trying to abort the baby I'm carrying because the father doesn't want it, and I already have one child. I didn't want another child out of wedlock."

Rafael looked at her in shock. "Mami, what did you say earlier to the nurse? You're pregnant? Ay… Dios mio." Rafael's eyes widened as he ran his fingers through his hair and stopped at the back of his neck. He couldn't believe what he had just heard, and all of a sudden felt so thankful that he brought her here instead of the doctor's office.

The nurse didn't seem at all surprised by Jocelyn's statement, but she did seem concerned, "Twelve weeks, huh? Well, let's get you in to see the doctor and see what's happening in there, okay? We're going to get you an ultrasound and then the doctor will tell you what's happening, alright?"

Jocelyn was barely listening, but felt grateful for

the kindness given to her by the nurse.

The nurse continued to give Rafael directions to the ultrasound area. "Follow the white line on the floor, give them this paperwork, and they'll tell you where to go from there."

Nurse Hampton was passionate about her job and knew how important it was to stay focused, so as she pointed she continued to call out for the next potential patient, "Maria Sanchez, Maria... Maria Sanchez."

There were so many people in the emergency room that Rafael didn't know how she kept so calm and caring. Nurse Hampton was obviously made for this job. He took the paperwork from her and proceeded to follow the white line, which led him to the ultrasound department.

The pain grew increasingly worse for Jocelyn, and her groaning became spontaneous screams and cries. The random rubbing of her stomach became more of a violent gripping as she bent over to bear it. By the time Rafael got to the ultrasound area, the nurse behind the desk was expecting them and took the paperwork. This was a miracle in and of itself. Normally there would be a very long wait. It was like someone knew they were coming and made a way.

Another nurse came from a hallway that was hidden by a wall, took the paperwork and said, "Follow me."

Jocelyn was terrified about what she might see. She hated hospitals, so she closed her eyes for fear of seeing something that would freak her out. "Don't leave me, Rafael...please."

"I won't, mami, I'm right here, don't worry."

The nurse saw how terrified Jocelyn was and said

to Rafael, "I'll take it from here, thank you," as she took the wheelchair from him.

Rafael tried to explain that Jocelyn asked for him to stay with her.

"I understand, and she'll be fine," she said as she escorted him out the door. "I promise I'll take good care of her. You just wait right out here, and she'll be done in no time."

He agreed reluctantly, feeling helpless. But he knew there wasn't much else he could do.

The ultrasound technician went back to Jocelyn who was hunched over in the wheelchair. "Listen, honey, I know you're in a great deal of pain, but in order for us to find out how we can help you, we need to do an ultrasound, okay? So I'm going to get something for you to drink and then after a while we'll see what's happening in that tummy of yours." The technician left and came back quickly with a tall plastic cup full of water that would help her see what was happening in Jocelyn's stomach.

Jocelyn drank it down completely. It actually felt cool and soothing instead of the burning sensation that went down her throat just hours ago. After a while, the technician came back and helped her onto a table that was right next to the ultrasound machine and asked her to pull up her shirt.

"This is going to be a little cold, okay?"

She was right. The techncian squeezed a cold gel-like substance onto Jocelyn's stomach. She then placed the roller on the gel and began to move it around. The technician was very focused on the screen. Jocelyn looked at her face, since she couldn't see the screen, to see if she could read her at all. She was looking for an expression of some kind…any kind…just something that would tell her that the baby was really gone. She felt terrible for thinking like that, but she had come this far and, after everything that had happened, she was hoping she still had a chance to fix things with Devon.

The technician continued to do her job, freeze-framing some of the screens for the doctor to see. She was almost done when she pressed down a little hard on Jocelyn's stomach.

"Oww!"

The technician looked at her with concern. "What are you feeling?"

"Sharp pain!"

"Okay, we're done here anyway, sweetie." She gave Jocelyn a few pieces of paper towel and told her to wipe off the gel, and then tried to help her back into the wheel chair. "Get up slowly now. Don't rush, take your time."

Jocelyn held her breath and got back into the wheelchair.

The ultrasound technician opened the door and Rafael was standing right there with a look of relief.

"How's she doing?"

"I need you to follow the green line on the floor to emergency care and bring her file with you. We will send the ultrasound pictures to the doctor on-call over there, and he will speak with her about what's happening, okay?" The technician looked down to Jocelyn with a compassion she wasn't used to. "You're doing great, sweetie, and I wish you all the best."

Jocelyn wondered why everyone was being so nice to her. Did they know that she had just drunken turpentine, whisky, and some other concoction just to abort her baby? Didn't they think she was a horrible person? The nicer they were, the worse she felt. She didn't deserve this kindness. She should have been put in jail just for what she did, and all she could think about was getting back with Devon. Jocelyn felt confused and detestable, both at the same time. Why couldn't she go to sleep and wake up realizing this was all a dream?

Rafael was talking to her as he followed the green line on the floor to the emergency care area of the hospital. Jocelyn heard his voice but didn't hear a word he said.

"Don't worry, mi amor, you're going to be just fine. I was praying for you the whole time you were in that ultrasound place. I know everything's going to be good. Okay, here we are." Rafael opened the door, held it with his foot, and pushed her through.

They approached the nurse's station with the clipboard that held her information. Jocelyn felt like she had been at this hospital for hours when she had really only been there for forty-five minutes at the most. The head nurse at the station took the clipboard and directed Rafael to wait for the doctor in an area where there was a bed and a chair. "The doctor will be with you shortly, y'all can take a seat over there for now."

Rafael wheeled Jocelyn into the area where everyone was waiting to hear something from some doctor. Finally the nurse called Jocelyn's name and directed them to a spot that was surrounded with a mint green curtain and a bed-like gernie. Rafael helped her up on the bed and pulled the half of a curtain across for what little privacy they could get in the small space.

Jocelyn was weak from bearing the pain in her stomach. She immediately turned on her side. "You must think I'm crazy, Rafael...but for what it's worth, I want to say thank you so much for being here with me and coming to my rescue. You're a good friend."

Rafael looked at her with disbelief. "I couldn't just leave you by yourself, mami. But why did you do this to yourself? You could have killed yourself."

"I wasn't thinking, Rafael. Devon is going to leave me if I have this baby…I love him, I can't lose him. I don't know what to do. I already have one child that I can barely take care of. Right now my son is with his godmother for the weekend, but I can't depend on them to help all the time. I'm a single mother on welfare and…well, you know what I do for a living. I can't bring another child into this life! Oh God, I'm so confused."

The doctor came in with the clipboard that had all of Jocelyn's information and her ultrasound pictures. He had gentle eyes, but Jocelyn was still afraid of what he would tell her. Rafael moved out of the way so the doctor was able to come close to Jocelyn, look into her eyes, and touch her hand. "You've had quite a day so far, haven't you? You wanna tell me why you chose to do this to yourself?"

"No, not really, just give me the bad news."

"Well, the bad news is you'll have to go through a psychological evaluation before leaving here, and if you were a singer you probably won't be able to sing much going forward. Now, every once in a while, as a doctor, I see what I like to call 'the hand of God.' Some of the other doctors call it luck. I choose to call it a miracle. The baby is miraculously fine, so is your placenta, but this is actually impossible given what you ingested."

Rafael exhaled, "Ay Gracias Dios."

Jocelyn was in shock and immediately felt all the blood in her body rush to her face. All of a sudden, it was like someone was pouring water over her head and it was running down her face. The tears came without warning and almost in a fury. She had no control. She was grateful for a second chance and was determined to do the right thing this time. All that could verbally come out of her mouth at this time was, "Thank you, God…thank you."

In a voice that matched his eyes, the doctor went on to say, "I need you to understand that turpentine can cause great damage in the digestive organs, inducing nausea, vomiting, and diarrhea. It can cause damage to the lungs, kidneys, and respiratory system. Not to mention this is something old ladies used to use in 'back rooms' a long time ago when women couldn't afford abortions. It would naturally induce an abortion along with other problems, but as far as what I can see, based on the ultrasound, everything is fine, and you're not twelve weeks pregnant, you're closer to fourteen weeks. That baby has to be here for a reason. I don't know what that reason might be, but there's gotta be a reason that we just cannot find. However, I want you to be aware of the very real possibility of the child having a mental retardation because of what you have done. It's too early to detect that now. After you're released from here, I want you to come back and see me in three weeks. As for today, we'll give you something to stabilize your stomach, but let me be clear, you *cannot* drink any alcohol while pregnant. Are you clear about that?"

"Yes, doctor, thank you so much."

"Okay, so we will be putting you in a room in a little while so we can assess your psychological stability before we release you."

"Wait, I have a son! How long will I be here?"

"It depends on how cooperative you are, but usually it takes a few days. Do you have anyone that can look after your son?"

"Well, he's at his godmother's now. I can ask if he can stay a few more days, I guess…"

"Okay, well do that, and we'll get you into a room as soon as we can."

"Thank you so much, doctor."

Rafael had a big smile on his face. "Mamita, you have a lot to thank God for. Did you hear him? He said you have a growing miracle in there." He touched her stomach. "Dios te bendiga. You're a blessed woman." Rafael felt compassion for her as he grabbed some Kleenex that was sitting on the makeshift sink next to the bed. He wiped her face and then put some in her hand. "Listen, mi amor, I'm going to go outside for a smoke, okay? But I'll be right back, don't worry."

Jocelyn nodded and said, "Thank you for being here, Rafael. Thank you. You don't owe me anything, and I feel ashamed even asking you, especially because you know what I do, but you're here and well…thank you."

Rafael kissed her gently on her forehead and quickly rushed to the door. "Two minutes, mama."

Jocelyn sat up in the bed and looked down at her stomach. She touched it with much care this time, ever so lightly rubbing it. She began to sob again as she mumbled, "I'm so sorry, little one. I didn't know what to do at the time…but I do now. You'll be okay, and I'll take care of you. Momma loves you. We'll be okay, I promise."

They say a promise is a comfort to a fool, but

Jocelyn meant that promise with all her heart at the time. She said it with all the guilt, shame, tainted love, and fear her heart could muster. She didn't know that this crisis would be one of many and that reliving the cycle would be a pattern she would master. She needed God more than ever. She never felt so alone in her life. When she felt like this she knew exactly what to do to soothe her pain, but this time she couldn't, at least not for the next five months. She would have to live with the feeling of being lost and feeling like shit for a while. She was going to have this baby, whether Devon would be there for her or not. Jocelyn was determined to make this very deeply scarred wrong right somehow. Out of a life full of alcohol, prostitution, rejection, low self-esteem, drugs, and ghetto living was going to come a life that God wanted, and for some reason that gave Jocelyn a small sense of purpose, something she wasn't used to feeling and didn't know what to do with, except try to honour it. Life was going to be rough for a while, but she was determined to try to make things better for her, her son, and now her unborn child. Still sobbing and rubbing her stomach, Jocelyn laid back, closed her eyes, and prayed.

"God, please help me. I can't do this by myself. I'm not strong enough. I mess up everything. Please help me do the right thing by this baby. I'm so sorry for messing with your creation. Please…please forgive me and give me strength."

At that very moment, just as she was about to say "Amen," she heard a small voice say, "*It's a girl.*"

She opened her eyes, thinking maybe Rafael might have come back and was messing with her, but no one was there. "Maybe it's a good idea they do this psych eval on me, little one. Ha ha, I think I'm losing it."

Then she heard it again, but her eyes were wide open this time. It was like the voice was coming from inside her, but how? She knew she was having a girl. She didn't know how she knew, but she just knew it.

"At one of the roughest points in my life, God Almighty chooses to bless me with a daughter? One of the darkest times of my life, You choose to use this baby to shine Your light on me? I don't deserve her." With tears flowing again, this time with a hint of joy and hope, Jocelyn spoke to her belly. "Your name is Dymond, 'cause you are my little diamond in the rough."

Rafael came back in, rubbing his hands together like he was trying to generate some heat. "I just saw the nurse, they're coming to move you to a room, mama. Who you talkin' to?"

Jocelyn smiled and answered, "My daughter."

A Change Is Coming

*"Change ain't easy, but it does show growth.
Staying the same just reveals fear."*
~Dymond

O n May 13, 1970, Dymond Asianah Avila was born, weighing eight and a half pounds, at three o'clock in the morning. Jocelyn had kept her word to the doctor and drank absolutely no alcohol for the entire pregnancy. She felt clearer than she had been in a very long time. When Dymond was born, the first thing Jocelyn asked the doctor was, "Does she look okay? Is there anything wrong with her?"

The nurses and the doctor were busy sucking out mucus, cutting the umbilical cord, wiping blood off, and congratulating her on her new baby.

"You did good, sweetie. The baby looks like she's doing just fine."

Jocelyn wanted to be sure that her Dymond was alright. She remembered what the doctor had said about the possibility of mental retardation and was afraid that she might not be ready to take care of her. "How will we know if she…if she's…you know…"

"Are you speaking of the mental retardation that

you were afraid of when you came in? We won't be able to tell or see signs until she starts trying to roll over, crawl, sit up, or walk. It's much too early to tell. Right now, you have what seems to be a beautiful, healthy little girl. Just enjoy your baby and take good care of yourself."

"Umm...okay...okay then, if you think she's okay, thank you." Jocelyn looked over to the left where two nurses were weighing little Dymond and putting a hat on her. They took blood from her heal, and she was crying, but it sounded like a normal cry to Jocelyn. She laid back trying to catch her breath and allowed the nurses to do their job. The placenta came out in tact and everything seemd alright. Jocelyn said a silent prayer of thanks to God for bringing her this far and asked if He could please keep her little Dymond healthy. When she finished her short prayer, Dymond was being put in her arms.

Dymond had the most beautiful blue eyes Jocelyn had ever seen. "How did she get blue eyes when her father and I have brown eyes?"

One of the nurses laughed. "Genetics is like that sometimes; it can skip generations, you know. Maybe it was a grandmother or great-grandmother or aunt or something like that. She's beautiful, Jocelyn, congratulations again."

Jocelyn just couldn't believe she was given such a precious gift. Even though her mother was absent most of her life, she was determined to be the best mom she could be. She felt a new determination to go to church and become dedicated to stay at home. Devon had disappeared completely. He cut off his phone and was no longer coming to church. Jocelyn had gotten to know his mother and sister a little and kept in touch with them, but even they didn't know where he was. Jocelyn found out the day she woke up in vomit and blood that not only was she pregnant but Devon had been cheating on her with another woman. She had no idea how deep the love was. She found out it was a love-hate relationship, and the name of this woman that he had committed his life to was *heroin*.

She knew he was battling alcoholism like her, that's where they connected, but she had no idea the drugs went past a little weed to a hardcore drug like heroin. She found his needle on the floor that day, and when she confronted him everything started to crash down on her. She thought telling him she was pregnant would make him realize what he would be losing if he continued down that path. Heroin was his first love, and he wasn't ready to let her go, even though he knew she was destroying him, little by little. He shook her that day, violently, and said, "Abort that baby, or it's over."

When Jocelyn looked down at her new bundle of joy, she couldn't imagine giving her up for him. She couldn't believe she even thought of aborting her for that relationship. It's amazing what can happen in five months. Jocelyn felt like a new person. She had hope and knew things would be better now.

Antoinette came to visit her, bearing gifts. "Look at you, J! You look great!" She walked right over to the basinet where Dymond was lying quietly. "Oh, look at her! Is this the precious little gem I've heard so much about? Wow, you were right, J, her eyes are piercing."

Ann gently picked up Dymond and began to rock her and talk to her. "Look at you, lil baby girl, you're perfect, aren't you? Well, lil lady, you are here for a real purpose, and we will be here for you all the way." Ann looked over to talk to Jocelyn and saw that she had fallen asleep. She stayed a little longer and put Dymond back to sleep, then she wrote a small note for Jocelyn and left.

Rafael picked up Jocelyn from the hospital and surprised her with a car seat. He knew she didn't have the money to get one. She'd been trying to make a real change, and he wanted to help. He walked into the hospital room and saw that Jocelyn was already packed and ready to go. "Hey, mamita, how are you and little niña doing?" Rafael was whispering like he didn't want to wake up the baby. "You ready to go?"

"Yeah, we're just about ready to go. Is it too much for me to ask you to stop by Julian's godmother so I can pick him up?"

"No problema, mi amor."

Dymond started to cry a little. Jocelyn hushed her and rocked her to try to assure her she was alright. Rafael watched and was mesmerized. "She's beautiful, Jocelyn." He looked at Jocelyn in amazement. "Jocelyn, I've seen you try to change your life for your kids, and I think you're doing a good job."

"Thanks, Rafael, that means a lot coming from you. I know my past with you isn't exactly one that I'm proud of, but you have been there for me every time I've needed you, and you didn't have to be. I don't know how I'm going to ever pay you back. I've never had a customer become a friend before, but I'm so grateful for your friendship to me. Thank you."

Rafael looked down for a minute with a half smile. Jocelyn never realized how handsome he was. He was always very well groomed, smelled good, and had a smile that made her want to stay around him. She kept her thoughts to herself because she didn't want to fall back into the old lifestyle she was accustomed to. It would be easy to give herself to him, and she knew exactly what he liked so she felt confident that she would be able to satisfy him completely.

"There you go, lil mama." She secured Dymond into the car seat and let Rafael carry it. "I think we're ready to go."

They both sighed as they headed out of the room. The head nurse came in frantically, "I'm so glad I caught you before you left. You forgot to fill out the paperwork for your daughter's birth certificate and registration. I filled out your name and Dymond's name, now I just need the father's to send it in. So glad I caught you guys. Fill this out and then bring it back to me at the nurse's station, okay?"

"Uhm, okay, yeah okay. We'll bring it right out. Thanks." As soon as the nurse left the room, Jocelyn turned to Rafael. "Rafael, this is the last time I'm going to ever ask you for anything ...well, anything major. I need you to sign your name here, but as Devon. I was speaking to Devon's mother and sister, and they were saying since it's Devon's first baby, even though he's not here, it's still important that Dymond has his last name. I'll fill out everything, I just need you to sign it, okay? Please."

Rafael looked at the papers. "What the hell, they won't know who I am. Okay, sure."

Jocelyn pretended she didn't miss Devon, but deep down she was secretly hoping he would hear that she gave Dymond his last name and want to come and see his baby. Rafael signed it, and Jocelyn threw her arms over his shoulders. "Thank you, thank you, thank you so much. This means a lot to me."

Rafael hugged her back, a little surprised with the show of emotion over something so little. "No problem, J, anything to help."

They dropped off the papers at the nurse's station and left. Rafael drove extremely carefully and took twice as long to get back to the apartment building. The projects was rough, but Rafael made sure she was good before leaving. As Jocelyn walked him to the door, he turned to her and said, "J, I have to ask you a question, but I don't want you to answer right now. I want you to think about it and then let me know what you think." He looked around like he had lost something, and Jocelyn felt a bit weird.

"Okay, what's up?"

"I want you to think about us different than the way we are now…more than friends. I can help you with the kids, and I know we could help each other go to church together….you know. I wanna help you, but I have feelings too, so yesterday I was thinking why not give us a try?"

Jocelyn was a little surprised. She had felt a serious conversation coming about the nature of their relationship, but she just didn't know how much he was feeling her. It was a bit more than what she had thought. He was talking commitment, and as tempting as that sounded, he wasn't Devon.

"Rafael, I love you so much, but…"

"Don't answer me now. Think about it first and then after we'll talk about it again. Okay?"

"Okay. Thank you so much for everything, Rafael. I promise I'll think about it, and we'll talk later. Good night."

Going to church with Julian and Dymond, for the first time since coming home three months ago, had Jocelyn a little nervous. She was still getting used to being a single mother to a three-year-old and three-month-old, and it wasn't easy. She was also a bit nervous about what everyone would think since she had self-rehabilitated from alcoholism. She wondered if anyone would believe her; she struggled to believe herself every day. Antoinette helped when she could, but she had her own family.

Jocelyn finally got to the church. "Hey, Sister Samantha, how you doin', girl? Love that skirt, you working it, girl." Jocelyn maneuvered the car seat in one hand and baby bag and son in the other. Sister Samantha took the baby bag and Julian from her. "Thank you, sis."

"Jocelyn, it's so good to see you, we've missed you around here. Hi there, Mr. Julian. Have you been taking care of mommy and your baby sister?"

Julian was a child with lots of energy. He was jumping and skipping along as she held his hand. "Yep, I did. I helped mommy."

If Sister Samantha didn't hold his hand, he would have ran away in seconds, not to be found for at least ten minutes. Jocelyn sat the car seat down on the pew and sat next to it. She started to take off her jacket, but Dymond started to fuss so she immediately unhooked the seatbelt and unzipped the snuggly she had dressed her in. She pushed back the canopy of the car seat until it was all the way back and carefully lifted Dymond out of the seat.

"There you go, mama, now everyone can see your pretty dress."

Sister Samantha brought Julian over to her after allowing him to run around a bit. "Sit down with mom, Julian. Church is starting."

Church was uplifting as usual. Jocelyn felt encouraged to keep on living a clean life. The worship was amazing, and even though she couldn't sing like she used to, she still tried. She had accepted God's forgiveness and knew that He understood her heart, so she had no problem experiencing honest exchange with Him. After the sermon, she started to think about Rafael differently. She still didn't answer him, and he was being so patient with her. Maybe she should let him help her, love her…she definitely needed help. Her thoughts were interrupted by church members and friends coming to congratulate her on her new baby.

"Look at her, she's just precious, Jocelyn."

"Her eyes are beautiful."

"You look great, Jocelyn."

While everyone gathered around Jocelyn, she heard a voice behind her. It sounded familiar, but she didn't pay attention to it. She started to get Dymond dressed and secured her in her car seat when she heard the voice again. "Can I hold her?"

Jocelyn turned around to see Devon in an all white linen pants suit. He looked like he just walked off a beach somewhere because his skin was beautifully tanned. She saw him, and her heart dropped. Her stomach turned upside down. She forgot about all the progress she had made in the last eight months. She forgot about Rafael. She forgot about her commitment to God. All that mattered was that Devon was here and he wanted to hold his daughter. She acted like she didn't care. "Well, well, well, long time no see, stranger. I'm heading home now, so maybe another time."

"Please. Just for a minute, Jocelyn. I know I don't deserve it. I just want to see her, just for a minute, please."

Jocelyn took a deep breath. She took Dymond out of the car seat, then stood upright and turned around to face him. "Okay, but just for a minute."

All eyes were on Jocelyn as she handed Devon his firstborn child. Everyone in the church knew what had happened between Jocelyn and Devon. This was the first time they had seen Devon in almost a year, and they didn't know what frame of mind he was in. Was he high? Was he sober? Was there going to be a fight? They were ready to protect Dymond, Julian, and Jocelyn if they had to. They all watched intently as he held his daughter for the first time.

Devon was overcome with emotion and began to cry. "Hi, little one. Mom named you well, huh? My little Dymond. Look at you. You have your great-grandmother's eyes."

"Oh, that's from your family?" Jocelyn added to their conversation. "Okay, good to finally know that."

Devon sat down with Dymond and spoke very softly to her in Spanish. "Esta muy linda, mi niña, te amo con todo mi corazon." It sounded like he was apologizing for not being there for her birth.

Jocelyn didn't understand what he was saying, but started to cry when she saw the tenderness being exchanged between Devon and Dymond. She quickly looked away while wiping her tears. She couldn't afford to give Devon an inch of emotion. She couldn't understand why Dymond wasn't crying yet. He was speaking to her as if they had a language that only they understood. This puzzled Jocelyn, since this was Dymond's first time seeing her dad.

How could she know him? Why wasn't she crying?

Could they have formed a bond already? Impossible.

Jocelyn reached out to take Dymond. "We really have to go now." Devon handed her his daughter and, in doing so, gently rubbed her arm. It immediately reminded Jocelyn of the gentle touch they used to exchange.

He leaned over and whispered, "I missed you, J. I'm sorry. I was scared. This is the first time I've ever had a child, I didn't know what to do. Give me another chance, please. I'll do right. I'm clean."

Jocelyn didn't hear everything Devon said because there were people still trying to leave church, and it was very noisy. She did hear him say *"I'm sorry... I'm clean....give me another chance."* Then, in that moment, life changed, again.

Part 2

"It's All I Knew"

My Hood

*"Sticks and stones may break your bones, but
WORDS can change your life!"*
~Dymond

Every little girl has dreams, no matter where
in the world she lives. I'm no different. My
name is Dymond. I'm a beautiful Black
Latina who has an alcoholic mother and a father
addicted to drugs. I love both of them, but I can't
look to either one of them as a role model. It's a cold
world, and I had to get over that quickly. Popi left
when I was a little girl, but he would come and live
with us a few times after that; hence the birth of my
little brother Darrin. Mom learned that not only was
he a fiend, but he was also married. She believed
that one day he would leave his wife and be with
her. Pipe dream. He was a user. That's what he did—
use—and it wasn't just heroin. He used everyone
he could to get what he wanted. But that wasn't his
true self, that was 'that stuff' making him that way.
Whenever he would get serious about getting clean,
he would come and live with us. I thought that was
crazy, since Mom needed help herself. She had her
own demons that she was fighting, but she loved
him and believed that her love would be enough to

help him get clean and stay that way. Both of them were hurt, wounded, and blind, but I guess they meant well. It's too bad that having good intentions isn't enough when real change is required.

Whenever he would come through, I always felt loved. I just wanted to be around him; I wanted his attention. He would look at me strangely at times. I came to understand as I got older that it was guilt and regret. At the time, I thought something was just wrong with me, like maybe I wasn't dressed right or maybe my hair was jacked up or maybe I was just ugly to him. There were other times where his look said, "Daddy loves you," and I felt like the most important person in the world. I remember when he taught me how to whistle. I remember him telling me how much he loved me and how much he wanted to stay just before he left. He tried to calm me down and make me stop crying by saying, "I can't right now, mami, but don't worry, I'll come back soon, and we'll have lots of time to play."

I saw him twenty years later. I always knew deep down that Devon loved me the best he could, but his best just wasn't good enough. I didn't know it then, but I would look for my father's love in every man I'd have a relationship with for a long time, until I broke out of my shell. The day my father left was a day I saw a side of my mother that I didn't recognize. They were arguing in the bedroom, and he picked up his suitcase and headed to the door. I was in the bathroom when I heard the arguing and her screaming.

"Where are you going? What am I supposed to do with these kids? I can't do this by myself!"

By the time I came running out to see what was going on, he was already at the door. Mom was standing in front of the door, right in front of the locks so he couldn't open the door to leave. She was crying. I'd never seen both desperation and despair at the same time until that day.

"I have your firstborn daughter, and now I'm about to have your son, and you're just gonna leave us?"

Devon's face was different. There was no desperation or despair of any kind. His face was more determined and disgusted. He was leaving, and it didn't matter what Mom said. "How the hell do I know if you're pregnant with my kid? It could be anyone's, 'cause I know you be trickin' when I'm not around. Bitch, get out my way."

"What? I haven't been with anyone else, and you know it, Devon. I've only been with you, baby. Why would you doubt me?"

Devon got really close to her face, and his voice got really deep. "Because you're nothing but an easy lay. Now get…out…of…my…way."

Mom looked shocked and hurt by what he said. "Is that what you really think about me, Devon? After everything we've been through? After everything I've done for you…that's what you think of me? That's all you gotta say about me?"

Tears streamed down Mom's face as she screamed those words to him. I felt hurt for her, so I screamed too. "Popi, stop making mommy cry! Where are you going? Don't go. Please, don't go. I want you to stay and play with me!" I ran to him and cried, too. I felt obligated to help her convince him to stay.

He caught me as I ran to him and squatted down to my level. He looked shocked like he didn't know I was listening and that I even understood what was happening. He thought I was in the bathroom because that's the last place he saw me go, and that was his getaway moment. But when I heard the crying and screaming I had ran out of the bathroom and was behind him, watching and listening to the whole argument. Both of them were so involved in their own lives that it was always a shock when someone busted into their moment to say, *"Uhm, hello, I'm right here."*

He hugged me as I continued to beg him to stay and play, and reassured me that he wasn't going for long. It was just for a little while. He would be back. "I can't right now, mami. But don't worry, I'll come back soon, and we'll have lots of time to play."

I knew he was lying, so I held on to his neck tightly. I was determined not to let him go, then something happened that changed everything. While he was lying to me, I heard each lock on our door being slowly turned to the unlocked position. Click, click, click, click. And then mom opened the door and said in a voice that I'd never heard before, "Get out."

If looks could kill, Popi would have been finished right there. Her voice was deep, emotionless, and sure. There was no whimpering, no confusion, no desperate cry, just nothing but nothing. She was done giving her all to a man who thought nothing of her. She watched me crying and holding on to him, "You don't deserve her. You don't deserve our love. Come here, mama, let him go."

I didn't let go, I didn't want to. I was scared of what would happen to us if he left. He gently unclasped my hands and took my arms off his neck. My father put my hands together and looked me straight in the eyes and said, "Your Popi loves you, and I'm gonna be back soon, okay mamita? Don't cry." He kissed me on both of my cheeks and on my forehead, stood up, picked up his suitcase, looked at my mother who had a look of "I'm done with you" on her face.

He shook his head and mumbled, "I'm sorry," and left.

My mother closed the door and locked all the locks, just to make sure he couldn't come back. She did it with emphasis this time. When she got to the last one, she banged on the door with her two fists and screamed, "I hate you! I hate you! I hate you!" then turned around and looked down at me. "Dymond, you never depend on a man, never, baby. Always have your own."

I didn't know what to say to that, so I just kept quiet. My mother stood there, leaned up against the door, for what seemed to be a long time, just staring out into nothing. Then she walked past me and went into the bedroom. As she walked away, I turned and decided to look at what she was looking at for so long, and to my shock, there was Julian. He had been sitting on the couch the whole time, listening to everything, watching everything. I walked up to him to talk to him because his face looked different, and I saw a tear jump out of his eye and roll down his cheek. I wondered why he was crying. I never knew him to be emotional. I never knew him to be sad. Angry, yes. Jealous, yes. Controlling, fo' sho. But sad, *never*. I was confused and didn't know what to say.

I was still wiping the tears from my face when he asked, "Is he gone forever?"

Julian's question shocked me again because he sounded weak and vulnerable. He didn't want to believe it. He didn't want Popi to go away. He wanted me to say, "No, they were just arguing." But instead I said, with a bit of a hard New York edge, "Yup, he said he was coming back, but you know he lyin'."

Julian wiped his tears and stood up off the couch like he was going to do something. I thought he was going to start a fight, so I jumped back and got into my ready stance, but he did something different. He told me what he was thinking. "Good, 'cause I hate him now, and if I ever see him again, I'll kill 'em."

I knew my brother was angry most of the time, but I never heard him say he hated anybody. I was scared because I believed him. I went into the bathroom, locked the door, and got into the bathtub. I curled up like a ball and fell asleep. But before I fell asleep, I started to daydream of a totally different life than the one I was living. I fell asleep and dreamed and dreamed and dreamed. Yeah, Popi left, Mom was crushed, Julian was mad as hell, and Darrin was about to be born in a couple of months, but I wasn't about to let any of that get in the way of my dreams. Dreaming was the only way I could cope with the constant drama that was around me.

Popi left, and life was never the same; it changed for the worse. Mom drank more and was depressed even more than usual. She stayed out at parties longer—for two or three days on end sometimes. Julian and I fought more often, and because of that, I learned how to handle myself better, but I still couldn't beat him yet. One of the good things that happened was that we spent a little more time with TiTi Ann and her family. We would go there after church on Sunday. Mom would bring us there, and we would have Sunday dinner sometimes, and I was able to just be a kid and play. Julian never bothered me there. TiTi Antoinette's eldest son would always protect me and keep Julian calm somehow. I really didn't care how he did it; I just wanted some peace, so I was happy when we would go over there. I really looked up to him. As you can imagine, I had to grow up fast and learn some really inappropriate things, but it was all I knew.

I was physically eight years old, but mentally and emotionally I was fifteen. Growing up in South Bronx was a trip sometimes, but I didn't let it stop me from travelling far away in my dreams. I dreamed to survive. I would dream all the time, awake or asleep. If I didn't dream, I would have died in that hell-hole my family called a home.

I used to tell my friends at school all about my dreams. They'd say, "Oh please, Dymond, that ain't neva gonna happen for you or anyone else around here. Get real."

I didn't care about what they had to say. I knew that one day my dreams were going to be real and life, as I knew it, was going to be different.

When I'd dream, it was always in bright colours. Some of the colours I'd never seen before in real life, but in my dream they took my breath away. Let me tell you about this dream I had almost every night. In my dream, I was all grown up, married, and living in a beautiful home. I had three children, and there was happiness in every room. Family pictures were in different places throughout the house. Fresh flowers with those colours I was telling you about were on the kitchen table, and it was so weird because every time I looked at the flowers, I felt an incredible amount of joy. The joy forced my face to smile, whether I wanted to or not, and sometimes a small laugh came without warning. There was the smell of home-cooked food that flowed all the way to the front door with music that was playing in the background—old school joints like "Midnight Train to Georgia." Peace and love were felt everywhere. I was at the sink washing collard greens when I felt something brush over my feet. I ignored it and continued looking out the kitchen window that was right over the sink in my dream house. I was humming to the music and watching my kids play in the backyard, when I felt it again. In my dream it felt like something was tugging at my toes, but then I felt a pinch. I jumped out of my sleep to find a rat trying to climb into bed with me. I kicked the rat off and grabbed the sheet that was hanging off the bed so the rat had nothing to climb up with. I watched the rat scurry to a dark corner of the room where there was a small hole, and disappear. "What the hell! Mommy! Ma!" I looked around to see if my mother was home. I looked down the hall to the bathroom, but the light was off and the clock said 4:17a.m. The room was pitch black and still, except for the moonlight shining through the blinds from the one window in our room. We lived in a one bedroom basement apartment in an apartment building that was not being taken care of, and we had been left alone, again, in the middle of the night. Mommy was…wherever mommy was. For those few moments while I was dreaming, I had something this hood could never give me—secret hope, a vision that I was going to make happen one day.

I really had no idea where my mother was or who she was with, but I knew one thing—I wasn't going back to sleep anytime soon. I was wide awake, alone, and still trying to get that rat image out of my head. Being alone wasn't a new thing for me; actually, that's how I spent most of my time. The other half of the time was spent dealing with the anger and worry

I felt because of my mother's drinking and constant crying. Not to mention the strange men she allowed to mistreat her in ways I secretly promised myself I never would. I was taught to "never say never," but I said never to that.

Sitting up straight in bed, I pulled my knees to my chest and closed my eyes so I could remember my dream, over and over again. It calmed me down and helped me to think to myself, *I'm gonna have that dream one day, I don't care 'bout no stupid rat or these dumb-ass cockaroaches either. It's gonna happen for me. I'm gonna have a home, and it's gonna be full of love and music and bright flowers and happy times. Damm straight...it's gonna happen...one day.*

Then I heard people's voices by my window. Our window was at street level, so all I could see were shoes and the bottom part of somebody's legs, but I could hear all kinds of crazy conversations. That particular night was different, though. There were two men trying to open *my* window. They were trying to get in! This was the South Bronx, and the only kind of people that were out at that time of the night were drug fiends, prostitutes, or straight up thieves. I couldn't believe it. I was in shock. I'd never heard a conversation like that before.

"Come on, man...you can't even open a little window? You can't be that weak!"

"Man, shut up and just keep lookin' out and make sure no one's comin' behind me!"

The blinds were closed, so they couldn't see me. *Where is my mother when I need her?* I wondered. *Did she lock the window?* I was too small to check the window, and I couldn't take any chances. For all I knew, they could have been high, which meant they could do things to me and not even remember it tomorrow. *Forget dat! I ain't no punk.* I had completely forgotten about the rat, roaches, and water bugs. I jumped off the bed, ran into the kitchen, and ran right into a chair that almost took my breath away. I got to the sink and grabbed the sharpest knife I could find. I knew that it would be there because my mom never did the dishes. I'd never used a knife before, but I heard about those dope fiends, and I wasn't going to be the next little girl that the neighbourhood talked about. Hell no, not this little girl. I was only eight years old, but they picked the wrong apartment this time.

I looked at the knife like it was my new best friend. I prepared myself for what might happen.

Yeah, they want somethin' in here? I got somethin' for those dope fiends. They really gonna try to come in here and take our stuff and hurt me? They must be out they mind!

As I walked back to the room quietly to see if they were able to get in, I remembered something that made me freeze in fear. I forgot that I had left my baby brother in that room, sleeping in the crib! Now I had to go back into the room and get him. I thought I was going to pee myself. I was so scared, but I couldn't leave him. Darrin was my responsibility, and he was just a baby. Knowing that I might have to stab someone in a minute to protect myself and Darrin made me feel angry, determined, and terrified all at the same time. I whispered a prayer before turning the corner. "Jesus, please don't let nobody hurt me or my brother."

I turned the corner with the knife in my hand, ready to stab anyone that would try to hurt me or Darrin, but I saw nothing. Where did they go? The dope fiends, or whoever they were, had left because they couldn't get in. I guess Mom did lock the window before leaving, or maybe they just gave up. Whatever the reason, they were gone, and we were safe again. I exhaled all the air I was holding in my lungs and said, "Thank you, God," over and over. I looked into the crib and Darrin was still sleeping like nothing had happened. "Thank you, God."

I was so relieved that I didn't have to find out whether I could have hurt someone or not. Little did I know that life had a funny way of coming full circle, and later on I would find out, first hand, it wasn't that hard to do. I jumped back into bed quickly because I remembered all the other nasty critters that lived with me. I pulled the sheet all the way up so that the rat wouldn't have a chance to get up into the bed. Something felt weird, but I couldn't figure out what it was until I looked down and remembered that I still had the knife in my hand, and I was shaking like a leaf in a windy rainstorm. My hands, my arms, my legs, every part of me was shaking. I pulled my legs close to my chest to stop the shaking and told myself, *They ain't comin' back, Dymond, calm down.*

For some reason, I was still afraid, and I didn't feel like it was time to let the knife go. Maybe they might come back and break the glass, and if they did, I was going to be ready. It was almost 5:00a.m., and I was tired but too afraid to close my eyes. I knew I had to calm down eventually, so I sang to myself, and I fell asleep in minutes. For some reason, music always brought peace to me, and whenever I felt afraid I would sing.

"He's leavin'...(leavin')...on that midnight train to Georgia...leavin' on the midnight train to Georgia,

whoo hoo."

Singing always makes me feel the same way I do when I'm dreaming, so you know I'm singing most of the time. I would sing anything and everything, from Coca-Cola commercials to the Jackson Five, to "Mary Had a Little Lamb."

There I was, eight years old with a knife in my hand, ready to stab anybody who felt froggy enough to jump, singing myself to sleep. I knew there was a lot wrong with my life, but music made me forget all about that. Singing made everything alright, even if it was just for a minute, even if it was just to help me get through a frightening moment. No matter what craziness happened, I was going to keep singing and dreaming. Those fiends didn't do anything wrong; after all, that was just their way of saying, "Welcome to the neighbourhood." My hood. It wasn't anything like my dreams, but it was my life.

Family Ties

"Family loves, fights, supports, rejects, shapes, believes, forgets, remembers, and starts you on your destiny path, but you determine the direction." ~Dymond

Sometimes Mom would be there in the morning and sometimes she wouldn't. I used to cherish the times I would hear, "Dymond, time to get up! It's time for school, lil mama."

After all that drama the night before, I had sung myself to sleep and woke up to a voice saying something just like that.

"Dymond, wake up and get ready for school." The voice sounded familiar so I opened up my eyes, and before I knew it, there was a hand coming across my face to make sure I was getting up. I totally forgot that my older brother was sleeping in the living room the whole time. I had forgotten because he always brought pain with his presence, and I tried to keep my mind free from that kind of pain. But this morning he reminded me again that the pain was real and not going anywhere anytime soon.

"What's wrong witchu, Julian? Whatchu hittin' me for, stupid?"

"Git up!" he yelled as he walked down the hall to the bathroom.

I had fallen asleep sitting up, so my neck and back were killin' me. I rubbed my face and my eyes and barked back, "Where's Mom anyway?" as I wiped away the hardened sleep from the corners of my eyes.

"Not here, ugly, now git up and go wash your face and git ready."

I could have been wrong, but I chose to believe that Julian didn't want to be mean, he was just angry, like I was, and didn't know how to say it. He was angry that he didn't know his daddy, angry that he was hungry and there was no food in the house ninety percent of the time, angry 'cause Mom wasn't there again, angry because he felt rejected and unimportant. Julian hated school, but he went because it was the only place where he could get attention, even if it was in the principal's office. He went because it was a source of entertainment for him, and he was tired of being home alone and bored. He said, "School's better than staying cooped up in that apartment all the time anyway." So I knew when he said, "Git ready," he meant for school.

There were only a few things that Julian and I had in common. We both loved school—for different reasons—hated the hell-hole we lived in, loved music, and we had the same mama, that was about it. Julian took his anger out on me most of the time. Most days, I secretly lived in fear when Mom wasn't around, which was most of the time, because Julian would find ways to torment me. Most days…every day…the anger came in beatings and scare tactics that would mess with my head. He was older than me by three years, taller, and stronger. The only ways I could fight back were to outsmart him or lock myself in the bathroom till Mom came home, or until he went to sleep. Today I didn't have time to hide or fight back. I had to find someone to look after Darrin so I could get to school. That meant I had to go across the hall and find out if our next door neighbour, Rafael, could babysit.

Opening the door in my building was always a risk because there could be a number of things happening in the hallway. The good news was Rafael was just three steps across the hall, and he was someone I could trust because he had always been there for my mother. At one point, I thought he liked her, but he never made a move, and she always kept it respectful with him. It was strange because I was so used to seeing her be disrespectful with other men, just not him.

"Rafael! Yo, Rafael! Hey, yo, open the door, please." I banged on the door for a good five minutes, or maybe it just felt that way, before I heard all the locks being opened, one at a time. Rafael's girlfriend, Lisa, opened the door, rubbing her eyes like she just woke up. It didn't matter because she was a beautiful Puerto Rican woman who could have easily modeled or been on a glamorous TV show. She had long black hair that always fell on either side of her head perfectly, no matter which way she decided to tilt it. She had naturally high cheekbones that made her look like she was always happy, even when she wasn't, and dark brown eyes. Lisa was probably about a size four, but her culture curves made her look like a six. Back in the day, she had a habit that messed up her chances to do anything real with her life, at least that's what she told me. Now she was trying to 'get herself together' with Rafael.

She was definitely with the right person. Out of all the families I knew in the building, he was the only one I could really trust. He cared about us for some strange reason, knew me since before I was born, and always called me his little miracle. Lisa opened the door while trying to put on her bathrobe.

"Okay, okay, lil mami, I'm coming, hold up! What's wrong? Wha' happen?"

"My mother's not home yet, and me and Julian have to go to school. So could you and Rafael watch Darrin for us till we get back? I'll make all his bottles and give you diapers and Vaseline and extra clothes. Pleeease?"

Lisa rolled her eyes. "Your mama ain't home again? This ain't good, lil mami. Who's taking care of you guys over there? How long she been gone? She turned to tell Rafael who was at the door, "Rafael, it's Dymond."

"I'm takin' care of me and Darrin, Julian takes care of himself, and I don't know, a couple days maybe. Come on, please, I really want to go to school today."

Rafael came to the door, also pulling on a robe, and squatted down to my level. "Okay, my bright lil Dymond, but when your mom comes home you tell her I want to talk to her. Intiendes?"

"Okay, sure, no problem. Thank you, thank you, thank you so much, good lookin' out. I'll be right back."

I only had a few minutes to get Darrin out of the crib, washed up, and get a couple of bottles together—carnation milk and water. I grabbed some diapers and Vaseline and one change of clothes, just in case he spat up on himself. I felt bad leaving my little brother, but school, church, and Titi Antoinette's house were the only places where I could dream without interruption and be a kid, even if it was for just a little while. They were places where I could dream, stop worrying about everyone else, and just be me. Just Dymond. I loved learning, and my mind sucked everything in like a sponge, so there was no question whether I was going to school.

Darrin woke up when I ran back to our apartment and slammed the metal door. I got him out of the crib, and he held on to me as usual. As I got him ready for Rafael's, I sang a song to him that would make him smile and help him wake up in a good mood. *"ABC...it's easy as 123...come on, baby, it's doe rae me, ABC, 123, baby, you and me, boy... whooo."* I didn't always know the words of the songs I sang, but Darrin was only a year and a half so he couldn't correct me anyway. He laughed as he watched me dance and sing to him while I cleaned him up with a washcloth. I finished changing his diaper and pulled his shirt over his head while he tried to sing and dance, too. He was waving his hands and kicking his feet off the edge of the sink that I had him propped up on. I did all of that with the heart of a 'lil mama,' because I had to. I knew nothing else except to do what I had to.

I pulled on clothes from the day before, my Buster Brown shoes, and brushed the front of my hair that was already in two pony tails. "Okay, Popi, let's go see Rafael and Lisa."

I struggled to pick him up with all the other things and realized I was going to have to do it in two trips. I left his bag and picked him up, ran across the hall and banged on Rafael's door, again. Bang! Bang! Bang! "Rafael...Lisa, it's us. Open up."

Rafael opened the door with a smile on his face.

He was dressed in track pants and a t-shirt. He immediately took Darrin and started to play with him. "Hey, Popi. Como esta? Look at you getting so big…Lisa, look at him. I have all these toys for you to play with today. You see? We're gonna have so much fun." Rafael put him down, and Darrin went crawling to the toys. I immediately felt a sense of relief because I knew Darrin would be safe and loved. Rafael was an angel in disguise, and even though he had been through his own stuff, I knew that he had turned his life around and would take good care of Darrin, like he was his own.

I heard some people in my building talking about some of the things he had lost because of his old habit. He had a son once, but lost him because he let that white demon, cocaine, consume him. He didn't get to see him regularly—only once in a while—but he had all kinds of toys for him for when he did come over. I never asked him about it, I just knew that he was great with Darrin, and Darrin and I loved him, too. He never cried whenever I left him with Rafael.

I watched as he played with Darrin. "I've never seen my mother do that with him."

"Whatchu say, mamita?"

I didn't realize I was thinking out loud. I immediately caught myself and said, "Huh? I said it looks like he loves you. Let me get the rest of his stuff."

I ran across the hall, back to the bathroom, and grabbed all his stuff and shoved it in his baby bag. I did a little check out loud as I was picking everything up. "Okay…Vaseline, got it… diapers, got them… extra clothes, shirt, pants, undershirt…what else? Oh yeah, his food!" I remembered that on my way home from school the day before I had stolen a jar of Gerber pineapple food from the corner store. I also made two bottles of carnation milk and water that I had put in the fridge. I ran to the fridge with my hands full and grabbed those last three things and shot back over to Rafael's across the hall.

"Here's everything, guys. Thank you so much for helping me. I'll be home right after school, I promise."

Rafael gave me a worried look. "Yeah, well I'ma look out for your mother 'cause I need to talk to her, but in the meantime, go to school, mamita, and learn sumthin, okay?"

"I will. I'm just gonna grab my book bag, and I'm going right now." I left Rafael's and made sure the door was closed behind me by pulling on it with two hands 'cause it was real heavy.

As I turned around to get my books for school, I saw Julian run out of the apartment like a bat out of hell. He didn't even say goodbye, and I really didn't care. I went back into the apartment, closed the door, and took a deep breath. It was quiet and peaceful, but just for four seconds. I ran to the bathroom. I needed to finish getting ready. I brushed my teeth and tried to run a comb through my hair, but being half-Black, half-Puerto Rican was tough, and my hair was my biggest problem. There was no amount of water or Afro Sheen that could tame this hair of mine. It was a problem. "Ugh, I gotta go, and this comb is hurtin' my head! Forget this, man, I'm not doin' this."

I decided to leave it in the two pony tails that had me looking like a wanna-be Mickey Mouse, where birds could build a nest. But it was the best I could do at the time. I grabbed my book bag and shook it off so there were no roaches on it, and headed toward the fridge. I felt like a fool opening the fridge door, hoping that something would magically appear.

"Girl, you stupid, you know ain't nothing in that fridge for you." I mumbled underneath my breath. I slammed the fridge door and ran out of the apartment. I ran right past the rats that looked like they were fighting over a piece of moldy bread. I didn't have time to be afraid of them today, I was late. And school was important to me. I ran towards Grand Concourse, which was an easy run because it was downhill, so it made me feel like I was running with the wind. Nothing could stop me now. I felt free.

Then just as I got to the bottom of the street, about to cross, I saw Mom stumbling out of the corner store with a paper bag in her hand and what I'm sure was Champale. I ran up to her and said "Ma! What are you doing out here?"

"Dymond, baby, whatchu doin out here? I was just about to come bring you and your brother to school." She tried to balance herself and speak without slurring her words, but it still came out like she was hella drunk. She grabbed my hand like she wanted to bring me somewhere. "Let's go."

"No!" I yelled angrily. Then I caught myself. "I mean no, I think you need to go home and sleep, Ma. You look tired."

All of a sudden there was panic in my mother's eyes. "Where's Darrin? Did you leave him in the crib by himself?"

"What? No! Why would I do that? No, he's at Rafael's. So you don't have to get him till later on. Go sleep, Mom, okay? Just go sleep."

Her eyes calmed down and she leaned on me, her eight-year-old daughter, as she walked back up the hill. I helped her all the way back to the apartment and made sure she climbed into bed. I was really late now, but I wasn't giving up. I closed the door with two hands quietly because I didn't want Rafael waking her up and cursing her out just yet.

After I knew the door was secure and she was in bed asleep, I bolted out like I was racing in the Olympics. Those rats were gone, but again I didn't care. I didn't want everyone asking me why I was late, so I tried my best to get there as fast as I could. By everyone, I meant my teacher and the principal, Miss Burnell. I ran towards Grand Concourse, talking to myself, "It's just around this corner, come on, girl, don't stop. It's just across this street, run, girl. It's right over there, come on, make it!" I didn't look for red lights, and I wasn't trying to obey the Don't Walk sign. I dodged in and out of traffic and got there just in time to say, "I pledge allegiance to the flag…" I was out of breath and wheezing, but I made it to school. I had no way of knowing that this was the day that was going to change my life, forever.

You Betta Believe It!

"Know your truth."~Dymond

After I sang the national anthem with all my heart, eyes closed like I was singing in church, Miss Burnell called me out into the hallway. "Dymond, come here right now. I need to speak to you."

I didn't know what she wanted, but I guessed it had to do with me running into class huffing and puffing, looking like I just got out of a fight. Regardless, Miss Burnell was my home girl. She was the principal of Langston Hughes' Little People School, and even if I was going to get in trouble, it was cool as long as it was her. She was tough but fair. So as soon as I finished singing the song, I ran over to her. I wasn't too scared because, no matter what, Miss Burnell was one of the few people in my life that showed me she cared. I could dream out loud with Miss Burnell and not feel like I was crazy, she was really nice. She would look in my greenish-blue eyes and actually listen to me, every time. Even though she knew what was happening in my home, she never judged me. She had seen my mother come and pick me up late and knew, just by the way my mother carried herself, what kind of household I lived in. I would come to school looking like I just rolled out of bed, because sometimes I did, but instead of yelling at me, Miss Burnell would call a teacher over to comb my hair. It's funny, right after my hair was done, I would feel better about myself. Sometimes she would give me a small carton of milk and a pack of cookies because I looked hungry, and 99.9% of the time I was. Yes, Miss Burnell took care of me in ways my own mother didn't, so whatever Miss Burnell wanted, as far as I was concerned, I was willing to do. Whatever punishment I was about to get for being late and coming into class in such a disruptive way, I was willing to bear.

I walked in her office and clearly said, "Yes, Miss Burnell?"

"Dymond, I need you to memorize this." She handed me a piece of paper with a Langston Hughes poem on it. "This poem is very important, Dymond. You have to memorize it, okay?"

"Med-or-ize? What's dat"?

"Not medorize, memorize. It means you remember all the words that are on this piece of paper without looking at it. You keep the words in your memory and tell me them once you've remembered them. I know it looks like a lot of words to remember, but I believe in you, Dymond. You can do it."

I had never memorized anything in my life, but I knew I was going to try because it was Miss Burnell asking, and if she said I could do it, then there must be some truth to it. I trusted her more than anyone in school, and she had never steered me wrong before, so I was going do it. When I walked home that day, I didn't notice the winos or the drug dealers that used to make my heart beat fast with fear because my eyes were glued to this piece of paper with the poem on it. I had never heard of this dude Langston Hughes before, but the poem was cool. I was able to get to know a little about him through it.

"I'm gonna have to look up some of these words in the dictionary when I get home 'cause I ain't never hear anyone say dat before…but it sounds important."

Beep Beep! "Little girl, get out the street!"

I wasn't paying attention to the street lights, so I had walked right into the middle of traffic and almost got hit by a car. I bolted back to the sidewalk and put the piece of paper in my pants' pocket, huffing and puffing, scared half to death. I am not getting killed over this poem. I'll work on it when I get home. *Thank you, God, for protecting me. Good lookin' out.*

I was excited about this whole poem memorizing thing. It was new, and I wanted to see if I could do it. I ran past the garbage cans where the family of rats lived, like I did every day, took out my keys from my shoe, and started to open the three locks of our door. As I opened the last lock, I hoped that my mother was going to be there.

"Ma! Mom! You here?" I slammed the door shut and proceeded to lock it, just like I was told to. I ran into the bedroom where I left Mom that morning and found her clothes on the floor. There was an outfit that looked like it didn't win her approval because it was left on the bed. She was gone, again. "Come on, man, again? I'm hungry dammit!"

I almost started to cry from frustration, but I decided to hold back the tears. I remembered Darrin was across the hall at Rafael's, and I had to be cool so he wouldn't ask a hundred questions. I went to the bathroom, washed my face with a cold wash cloth, and headed back to the door to go across the hallway to get Darrin. I was glad Julian wasn't home yet; I wasn't ready to deal with him.

Knock, knock. "Hey Rafael…Lisa, it's me, Dymond."

Rafael came to the door and looked right past me down the hall. "Where's jur mother, Dymond, huh? Where is she?"

I had to admit to him that I didn't really know in a way that wouldn't make him worry too much. "I'm not sure right now, but I'm sure she'll be right back though."

"Dymond, you know I don't mind lookin' after lil Darrin, but you can't be stayin' by yourself all the time like this. Whatchu gonna eat for dinner tonight?"

"Not sure yet, but I am sure it will be yummy."

"Lil girl, don't play wit me!"

"I'm not trying to be smart with you, Rafael. I just don't know what to say."

At this point, I should have heard Darrin or he should have ran to the door or something. I looked in and saw him sound asleep on Rafael's couch. Before I could say anything, Rafael said, "He's sleeping now. I'll bring him over when he wake up and after I feed heem, okay mamita?" He hesitated a minute and then said in a whisper, "I would have you stay over here too, but Lisa and I are having a grown up talk. When we're done I come and get you so we can eat together, okay lil mami? Julian can come too if he's over there witchu."

I threw my hands around his neck and even though I didn't want to, the tears started to push out through the corner of my right eye. I held my breath and said, "Thank you, Rafael, thank you so much." I ran back across the hall into my apartment and locked the door. I ran into the bathroom and locked that door too just in case Julian came home. I didn't want to have to deal with him while I was feeling so emotional. I sat on the edge of the tub that was really in need of some Ajax or something, and put my hands over my face and just cried. I hated crying, but I couldn't help it that time. I wanted my mom. I was so hungry but at the same time so grateful for even the thought of someone giving me and Darrin food later. I started to talk to God because I was told that He's "always on the mainline, tell Him whatchu want." So I did.

"God, where's my momma? Why doesn't she care about us? Why do we have to live here with all these stupid rats and roaches and water bugs? And where's my popi? God, I'm tired of being hungry and scared and having to act tough all the time. Please help me, please. I'll do anything you want. I'll be a good girl, I swear, just please help me, God."

At the end of the prayer, I heard the door slam. It was either my mother or Julian. I quickly got up, rinsed my face with cold water, dried it with toilet paper, and then waited. If it was my mom, I would leave the bathroom, and I would thank God for the rest of the night for listening to my prayer and helping me so quickly. If it was Julian, I was staying in the bathroom a little while longer because I didn't want to be tormented by him. I put my ear to the door to try to listen to the noise on the other side. I couldn't hear anything. Then all of a sudden I heard Bang! Bang! Bang! on the bathroom door. I jumped back and put my hand over my mouth so I wouldn't scream out loud. I heard Julian's voice.

"Dymond! Dymond! You in there? Why's the door locked? Whatchu doin' in there? Open up!"

My heart was beating so fast that without putting my hand on my chest I could feel it coming through my shirt. I learned a long time ago never to show Julian how scared I was or he would use it against me. So in a calm voice I said, "I'm using the bathroom, man. Wait!"

"Well hurry up. I gotta pee!" he barked.

"You betta find somewhere outside 'cause I'm gonna be in here for a while."

"Aw man, come on, can't you hurry up? I really gotta go."

"Nope. Sorry." I heard him run towards the front door fast, and then I heard it slam. I exhaled and sat back on the side of the bathtub thinking, *I'll just stay in here till I hear Rafael knock, then I'll run to the door and go over there till mom gets home.*

After about a minute, I heard a huge kick on the bathroom door. BANG!

"What are you doing?" Julian was back, and he was mad. He knew I wasn't using the bathroom, and now he was trying to kick down the door. "I need to use the bathroom, stupid! Now open this door!"

"Only if you stop banging."

"Oka-ayah, just hurry up, man!"

I flushed the toilet, committed to playing this role to the end. I went to the sink to wash my hands and didn't bother drying them, just to show I was trying to hurry up. Then I took a deep breath and opened the door. Julian was ready for me. His fist met my face quicker than I had anticipated, and I was down on the ground before I knew it. "Get out!"

I'm not sure how I got up. I ran outside because I couldn't wait for Rafael to knock on the door. I had to get away from Julian. He was angry, and I was going to be his punching bag for the rest of the night. I went across the hall and knocked on Rafael's door like my life depended on it. "Rafael, it's me, Dymond. Please open up…Rafael!"

I kept looking behind me to see if Julian was going to open the door and catch me. He knew I had a good relationship with our neighbours, but I didn't know if he would come out of the apartment and act up. Rafael opened the door and looked at me, confused. I jumped in his apartment before he had time to respond.

"I told you I would come get you when I'm done, lil mamita. Wha' happen?"

"I wanted to help you with dinner. Don't mind me, I'll be invisible, and I won't even listen to you and Lisa's conversation, I promise. I just wanna be over here with y'all. Okay?"

"You are actin' weird, but okay, come in."

Darrin was still asleep. I decided to lie down next to him. I didn't realize how exhausted I was. I didn't sleep much the night before, so it made sense that I was tired.

"Where's Julian, Dymond?"

"He's over there actin' up. He wants to be by himself for a while."

Rafael understood at that point why I came back over, why my face looked so red, and why I wanted to help with dinner. "Okay, mami," he looked sympathetic. "Lie down with your leedle brother. We cook in a leedle while."

As I rested on the couch, I remembered my poem and took the paper out of my pocket. I fell asleep reading it over and over. The poem was called "I Dream a World." As I read it, I felt like Langston

Hughes knew me personally. He dreamed of a world where men weren't judged by race, and he wanted to feel free. I was only eight years old, but I knew how it felt to want freedom because I felt trapped every day. Miss Burnell saw something in me that made her believe I could memorize a part of this poem. I had never done it before, but I believed in her, and the way she cared about me made me loyal to her. So I fell asleep trying to memorize those words, and then it started to happen without warning. I started to dream. I dreamed that maybe, just maybe, Miss Burnell was right and I could really do what she said I could. Then I was on stage with a mic in my hand doing the poem, but I sounded different. I sounded confident and even special in some weird way. I didn't know what it was that made me feel special, but in my dream I was sure about it. Deep down in my heart I knew it. I was special in my dream, I believed it.

I See

"What you believe to be true has nothing to do with what you see. Don't be fooled, it's all about your perspective." ~Dymond

When I woke up, I quickly realized that I was back in my apartment and in bed. Rafael must have picked me up off his couch and taken Darrin and me home. I was so tired I didn't even feel the transfer. I turned over to look and saw that Darrin was fast asleep in the crib. We lived in a one bedroom apartment, and Mom, Darrin, and I shared a room, while Julian slept on the pullout couch in the living room. I sat up and looked around the room to see if my mom was home. She wasn't there, as usual, but I heard noises in the kitchen. I looked over the edge of the bed to see if there were any roaches or water bugs and then quietly slid off to see who was in the kitchen. If it was Julian, I didn't want him to know I was awake because I wanted to hold on to the little peace I had for as long as I could. I peeked around the corner and looked into the kitchen.

"Hi, Ma!"

I couldn't believe it...Mom was in the kitchen, and it looked like she had gone to the store. She was actually cooking something for us to eat. I ran to her, thankful she was home, so I wouldn't have to deal with Julian by myself today. I hadn't seen her since yesterday when I helped her get into the apartment and laid her down in the bed and didn't know if anything bad had happened to her or even if she was coming back.

"When did you come home? We missed you." I was confused. What was really going on? *Did she pick me from Rafael's? Did she come home late and see me already in the house?* At this point I didn't care, Mom was home. We were about to eat food, and I didn't have to worry about defending myself from Julian.

"Hey, my little Dymond, sleepyhead, you ready to eat something before I walk you to school?"

"Yep, I'ma get Darrin and wash up, okay?" I was actually telling her rather than asking. I ran back into the room, still looking for roaches and water bugs on the floor since they came out whenever they wanted to and I couldn't bear to step on one. After seeing that the floor was clear, I walked up to Darrin's crib, lowered the edge and then threw on the light. I saw some roaches in the corner of the room scatter under the bed, but I didn't care. I had to get Darrin and myself together so I wouldn't be late for school. I started to pat Darrin's back.

"Darrin…Darrin…popi…wake up." I picked him up, and his diaper was soaked. He was getting heavier and bigger, but I was so used to handling him that it wasn't a problem for me. I put him on my side and reached under the crib for the Pampers bag, grabbed a diaper, and then headed into the bathroom. "Did popi have a good sleep? Huh, baby? You're such a good boy."

We got into the bathroom, and normally I would sit him down so he wouldn't fall over, but this time I put him to stand up by himself. He was learning how to stabilize himself, so I didn't have to worry about him falling. I grabbed a washcloth that was over the tub faucet, took the ivory soap, and rubbed the cloth and the soap together, then put it at the edge of the sink. I took off the undershirt that he was wearing and his diaper that had held all of his night urine. He stunk, and I had to get my baby smelling right.

"Whew, popi, you're killin' me. Come on up here and sit on the edge of this sink so I can clean you up." The sink was high or I was short, either way it was always challenging getting him cleaned up. I got on my tippy toes and made it happen. I washed him up and put on the clean diaper. I had to lay him on a towel on the bathroom floor to change him. After applying a healthy helping of Vaseline, I carried him back to the room to find some clothes for him to wear. I placed him back in his crib. "Sit, popi, don't move." I ran over to the dresser and found socks, pants, and a shirt that looked like he should be on Sesame Street; it was definitely a shirt that Ernie would wear—red and orange stripes. He didn't care, he was just happy that I was taking care of him. I was hoping that along with the food, Mom remembered to make his bottle because he was going to be hungry. If she didn't, my backup plan was to let him eat my breakfast, so he would be good till the afternoon.

"There, popi, look at you. So clean and handsome. You're such a good boy. Come on, let's see what Mom is making. You wanna see Momma?"

"Momma." Darrin didn't talk much, but he did

copy me sometimes. I took him out and sat him on the bed, then looked underneath the crib for his shoes. They were under the crib. I bent down, grabbed them, and shook them upside down to make sure no roaches were chilling in there. I took him off the bed and stood him up on his own two feet, then I took Darrin's hand and led him out of the room into the kitchen. Mom had already put pancakes on the table and she even made Darrin's bottle. I put Darrin in one of the kitchen chairs and started to put his shoes on when Mom took them from me.

"Go 'head, Dymond, eat something. I'll put his shoes on."

I realized she might have felt a little guilty since I was the one taking care of Darrin when she wasn't home. I stepped out of the way and let her do whatever she wanted. I hadn't heard Julian at all and looked over in the living room and saw that he was still sleeping. "Ma, Julian ain't going to school today?"

"Yeah, he is. Julian, get your behind up out of that bed and get ready for school, boy."

Julian was such a heavy sleeper. You would think he would have woken up when she was cooking, but no, not him. He was still sound asleep. I went over to his bed, which was also our couch, just pulled out. He was sleeping on his stomach with his hands at his sides. I knelt down and started to rock him back and forth.

"Julian! Julian! Julian, man, wake up! Wake up, man. It's time to get up. We gotta go to school."

Julian seemed unusually tired. What I didn't know then was that after school he had been hanging out with his bestfriend, Keith, and they had been running up and down in the streets all night. Julian took his left hand and shooed me away. "Leave me alone, D." It's amazing how, even half asleep, his one hand pushed me hard enough that I fell back.

I went back to the table to eat because I didn't know when I was going to get this again, and I wasn't about to miss it. By that time my mom was in the chair holding Darrin, feeding him his bottle. She turned and yelled one more time, "Boy, get up out of that bed before I come over and get you."

He got up slowly. "Alright, man, stop yelling at me."

Mommy was rough with him. "We're leaving in fifteen minutes, and you betta be ready. I cooked pancakes for y'all, now go wash up and come the hell on!"

Julian heard pancakes and automatically came to life. I hadn't had time to wash my face or brush my teeth, so I ran into the bathroom before it became a fight. I wasn't going to be late for school again, and today was going to be different than yesterday. I could feel it. It had already started off like I was in a dream. While running to the bathroom to finish washing up, I pinched my arm to make sure this was real. My skin turned pink and it hurt, so either this was the most realistic dream I'd ever had or this wasn't a dream and we were having a good day. I didn't know what was going to happen after school, but I knew at that moment that I was grateful I wasn't going to school hungry. When I got into the bathroom, I looked at myself in the mirror and said, "This is not a dream. Things are gonna get better."

At that moment, I didn't know what it was, but I felt like there was a reason for me to have hope. Maybe it was the dream I had at Rafael's house that made me feel like I was something special. Maybe it was the poem I had to memorize that had my mind thinking of a better world. Maybe it was the fact that my mother was here with us and acting like a mom. I didn't know what it was, but I knew it wasn't a dream. I had hope. For the first time in a long time, I had hope. I was going to eat those pancakes and head to school, and it was going to be a great day because I was able to see things differently. It felt like I was seeing things for the first time, even though I knew I wasn't. I didn't know at the time that I was just viewing things from a perspective of hope. There were random times when my mom tried to get herself together and be a good mother for us. She tried at different times. They didn't last long, but what they did for me lasted longer than the memory. What it gave me was the ability to see what my future could look like. It helped me shape my perspective, and even though I wasn't sure how long this moment would last, I was sure about one thing, now I could see.

Part 3

"A Change Is Gonna Come"

Mountains & Valleys

"We have to grow; it's inevitable. What we feed our souls will determine which way that growth will take us. Bon appetite." ~Dymond

Mom walked us to school that morning, but for some reason she was walking slowly. I don't know if she just wanted to take her time and talk to us, or if I was just excited to get to school, but I know she had to yell at me to slow down at least four times. Julian walked with us halfway and then he went the rest of the way by himself. He went to a different school from me. I was really happy about that, even though I knew next year we would be in the same school. For now, school was my sanctuary, the place where I experienced peace and was able to just be myself and learn. We said goodbye to Julian as he ran off toward his school, fixing his book bag on his back and trying to tuck in his shirt. We kept on walking. I went to C.E.S. 236 Langston Hughes Little People School. It was the best place in the world. School, church, and Titi Antoinette's house, those were the three places where I could act my age and be a kid. I was able to learn and laugh and just experience life the way an eight-year-old should.

Mom was asking me all kinds of questions and acting kind of weird, but I didn't have time to investigate the motives behind it. I had to see Miss Burnell.

"Dymond, girl, if you don't slow down…come here and hold my hand, child."

"Hold your hand? Ma, I gotta get to school, and I can't be late today."

Mom was carrying Darrin so I didn't know how she intended to hold my hand. And since when did holding hands become a part of the way we interacted? She was throwing me off, but I had to stay focused. I just knew today was going to be different. I wasn't sure how it was going to be different, but I just felt it in my stomach.

"Ma, I see my school! I'm gonna run, okay?"

"No, Dymond, wait for me. I want to make sure you get in the school yard safely. These people out here driving like there ain't nobody but them on the road. You just hold on." She was killing me, but it wasn't every day that she walked us to school, so I let her catch up. That day my hair was combed, my clothes were clean, I'd had breakfast, and my mother was walking me to school. So it was alright for me to wait for her. At least she wasn't like some of the other mothers that would drop off their children to school looking all crazy like they just rolled out of bed. One thing I will say about my mom is that even though she was dealing with some issues, she always knew how to put herself together. She was a slim framed woman with beautiful, smooth, caramel skin that was soft to the touch. She had dark brown shoulder length hair and brown eyes. Her nose and lips were very thin like white people's (probably because her grandmother was white). Mommy was different though, she was one of those Black people that would say stuff that would make you think she didn't like her own people sometimes. She would say stuff like, "Black people are just ignorant, Dymond. You gotta behave yourself and know how to talk to people. Don't be yelling and carrying on like some of these crazy negros out here." I would always listen, but never really understood what she meant. Not until I got older did I realize that she didn't want to be boxed into the stereotype that portrayed us as loud, lazy, and looking for hand outs. She was one of those Black women that wanted to be judged by the content of her character, not on the pigmentation of her skin.

At the time, I would just be quiet and listen out of respect. Even though I didn't see Mommy often, one thing I did learn very quickly was that she was a woman you were going to respect. At least, as children, we tried to when she was around. Now let me be clear, we didn't respect what Mommy did or how she lived, but we did fear her and the authority she had over us as children. It made even Julian walk the chalk line when she was around. Even though she had a very feminine, dainty way about her, she was still Mommy, and we gave her the respect that she was due, or else we felt the wrath of the belt.

Yeah, she stood out in a crowd. She was beautiful, and as we walked to school, even with Darrin propped up on her left side and me holding her hand on the right, she still had it. The 'it' factor made her stand out because the Black women in our hood were a bit rough and downright masculine sometimes. It was mostly because the fathers were missing-in-action or just didn't know how to step up and take care of their business, which left the women doing what needed to be done, and then some. The Black women in my hood didn't have time to get their hair done, unless it was a special occasion. They didn't always take the time to put themselves together, unless it was for work. The Hispanic women would always look tight, but had language issues, and that kept them in the house with their families most of the time. They were Mommy's real competition. Those Spanish curves had a language all their own, and salsa and meringue music walked with them. With all that said, my hood did have a lot of people that were battling some inner demons they didn't know how to get rid of. Mommy was too, but she just knew how to dress that demon up. She always had her hair done, and her clothes looked like she should model for Vogue. It was probably because she sewed all her clothes and wouldn't use any patterns except for Vogue. She had an elegant sophistication about her that moved with her as she sauntered down the street. It was rare and stood out. All kinds of men noticed it all the time. Men in cars would honk and yell stuff like, "That must be jelly cause jam don't shake like that!" or "Oye, muy leenda, mami!" Men walking with their women would turn and stare at my mother, even though they knew they would catch a case because of it. Yeah, Mommy had it like that so I didn't mind her walking me into the school yard.

We crossed the last street, and I shook her hand loose and looked at her.

"Go ahead," Mom said. "I see Miss Burnell, have

fun."

I ran like I stole something. I saw Miss Burnell and couldn't wait to tell her that I memorized the whole poem. Before I knew it, I ran right into her and hugged her. She took a step back, not expecting the thrust to be so forceful.

"Oh my goodness, well good morning, Dymond. And how are we today?"

"We are great 'cause we medorized the poem!"

"You mean memorized."

"Yeah, yeah, mem-mor-ized, that's what I meant."

"I can't wait to hear it. Now, in you go, you have about five minutes to play and then the bell is going to ring."

I turned to see Mommy right behind me. "Bye, ma!"

"Bye, baby girl, see you after school. Good morning, Miss Burnell."

"Miss Day, how are you? I haven't seen you in a while, all is well?"

"Yes, yes, all is well. I had some things that I had to attend to for a couple of days, but yes, everything is good now."

As I walked away, I was curious to know what those 'things' were that kept her away from us for three days, but I would have to figure that out later. I was in the playground, and I saw my best friend, Tatyana. She had the biggest afro in school, but she was the most loyal and the most fun, so I didn't care that it hit me in the face more times than I could count. I ran over to her and saw that she was already in a heated game of kiss-n-tag with Ricky.

"I wanna play. Who else is playing? Where's Geraldo and Pierre and Gregory?"

"They over there! Girl, run! Here he comes...

aah!"

I started to run with her, trying to see who else was playing. Then I spotted Geraldo and Pierre leaning against the wall, talking. They saw we were playing kiss-n-tag and immediately wanted to join. A few other girls wanted to join us too but they didn't have a chance with me and Tat in the game. Secretly, I wanted Geraldo to kiss me, but I had to play it hard. I really didn't know what I would do if he caught me, but there was something inside me that was excited to find out. Just the thought of him kissing me was enough to have me giggling like a fool for no reason.

We ran up the stairs and slid down the slide, and there he was at the bottom, waiting for me. Pierre. Pierre was a Puerto Rican kid who was told by his parents not to play with me. Well, at least, that was what he whispered to me once when we were in class, after I asked if I could sit next to him. "I can't sit next to you because you're Black, and my mom knows your mom. She said I shouldn't talk to you, sorry."

I acted like it didn't matter, but it did. He was at the bottom of the slide, and before I could get out of his way, he grabbed my hand. "Gotchu!" he said as he kissed me on the cheek. "I don't care what my mom says, your eyes are beautiful, and so are you."

I felt my face get warm immediately, so I pulled away to get out of his grip. "Thanks."

I continued to play the game, but for me the game was over. I had gotten what I wanted, and now a new game had just begun.

Tatyana came running behind me screaming, "Run, Dymond! Goooo! They're coming!" We ran together to try to get away from the boys, and then the bell rang. I went over to pick up my book bag that I had thrown down at the side of the playground, and then went to line up. As we were walking in, I saw Pierre looking back at me, mouthing something. Tatyana was right in front of me, so I could hardly make out what he was saying, because her hair was in the way. She turned and said, "Don't you see Pierre talkin' to you girl? He said sit next to him today."

"I see him, and I ain't sittin' nowhere near him today, he buggin'." I wanted to, but I couldn't let him feel like he could just tell me something and I would jump to it, oh no. I would eventually sit next to him, just not today. As we all got into class and took off our coats and put everything in our cubby holes, I asked Miss Williams if I could go see Miss Burnell for a quick second. I ran out of class so fast I didn't even notice Pierre's disappointment, nor did I care at that moment. It was all about showing Miss Burnell that I had done what she had asked. Miss Burnell was standing in the front foyer of the school waiting patiently for the late stragglers. She always said, "Good Morning!" with the biggest smile, whether you were on time or late.

"Miss Burnell, I did it, I medorized the poem last night, and I know it off by heart."

"Very good, Dymond! I knew you could do it. I can't wait to hear it, go wait for me in my office. And it's mem-or-ize."

I skipped to her office that was only five feet away and sat in the only chair there aside from the one behind her desk. I was always captivated by the pictures of her family on her desk and the books on her book shelf. There was everything from Dr. Seus to Alex Haley. She had awards and certificates on her wall that commended her for her life's work and community service. I was reminded, while sitting there, of her amazing character as a mother, teacher, educator, student, and community servant. She was just the bomb, and I wanted to make her proud. As she walked into her office, she mentioned, "It was so very nice to see your mother this morning with your little brother."

Under my breath I mumbled, "Yeah, she surprised me, too."

"Huh?"

"Nothing. Can I say it for you now?"

"Of course. Wait, wait, let me sit down for this." She settled into her seat and got comfortable. "Okay, lil Dymond, go for it."

I jumped off the seat, carefully clasped my hands together in front of me, cleared my throat, changed my smiling face to focus, and began.

"I dream a world where man
no other man will scorn,
Where love will bless the earth,
and peace its paths adorn,
I dream a world where all will know
sweet freedom's way,
Where greed no longer saps the soul,
nor avarice blights our day.
A world I dream where black or white,
whatever race you be,
Will share the bounties of the earth,
and every man is free,
Where wretchedness will hang its head,
and joy, like a pearl,
Attends the needs of all mankind—
Of such I dream, my world!"

Miss Burnell jumped out of her seat and came out from behind her desk. "Dymond, how did you memorize the whole poem? Oh my goodness, you were only supposed to memorize the first eight lines. I'm so proud of you! Good girl!" She picked me up and hugged me tightly. It was like we did something great together and had reason to celebrate. "Wonderful, just wonderful, Dymond! Now here's what I need you to do. I only need you to repeat the first eight lines, and Pierre is going to say the last eight lines. Both of you will recite this together in front of some people at a school on Thursday, okay?"

"Hold up…in front of who, Miss Burnell? And how am I gonna get there?"

"Don't you worry yourself about that, honey. I'll pick you up at 6:30pm on Thursday, you just put on your best dress, and I'll take care of the rest, okay? I'm so very proud of you, Dymond. Very good. Okay, back to class you go."

My heart was full. I felt like what just happened didn't really happen and that I was dreaming, so I pinched myself, again. It hurt, and my skin turned bright pink, so I knew it was real. I had never had an adult proud of me before, and I really didn't know how to take the compliment, but even without my mind knowing how to process it, my heart knew and was beaming with joy. I skipped into the classroom and went through the day like I was walking on a cloud.

When I got back into the classroom, everyone was getting up and heading to different places to learn different things. Miss Williams called me over to a table. "Come over here, Dymond, you're going to play the memory game with everyone."

I started to walk over to the table but then spotted Pierre. "Ay, yo! Go see Miss Burnell, she has something to tell you."

"About what? The poem?"

How did he know? "Yeah."

"I already know we're gonna say it together this Thursday."

I was a little confused because I didn't know that he knew before me. I guess Miss Burnell had this all planned out. It was cool with me because I trusted her completely.

The day went by fast. I learned a lot, and it seemed like everything I did was with greater pride, effort, and diligence. I felt like someone put an extra squirt of special in my carton of milk, and I was using all that special energy up with everything I did.

After school, I waited for my mother to come and pick me up. I knew she liked to saunter instead of walk and that she had Darrin, so I decided to play in the playground until she came. I was the last person in the yard. Miss Burnell looked at her watch and then looked at me. "You stay right there, lil Dymond, I'll get my things and take you home. I'm sure there's a very good reason why your mom is late, again."

This was a normal thing, but for some reason today I thought things were going to be different, I thought she was going to be different. "Okay, Miss Burnell."

When she went into the school, I picked up my book bag and ran all the way home. I didn't want her to see where I lived, and to be honest, my part of town wasn't friendly or kind to white people. I didn't want anything to happen to her, so I went home on my own, thinking I'd make up a lie the next day and tell her my mom came the minute she walked inside. When I got home, I felt the special juice wearing off. I didn't know what to expect, and I had to get my mind ready for Julian. Who knew what kind of day he'd had. I knocked on the door, Mom answered it, and she didn't look that great.

"Ma? What happened? Miss Burnell and I waited for you at school…"

She looked up at the clock on the wall. "Oh shit, I mean shoot, shoot, I'm sorry, baby. I lost track of time."

She closed the door and locked all the locks. I went into the room and saw that Darrin was sleeping in the crib. Julian wasn't home yet, and there was a man in my room fixing his pants.

"Dymond! Come on out here and watch this TV, Mommy has a guest who's just leaving."

I backed up out of the room and looked at my mother with tears in my eyes that I would not allow beyond the rim. I went to the bathroom, locked the door, and turned on the water so no one would hear me cry. My mother had chosen another random dude over me. Why? What did I do wrong? I had such a great day at school. Was it that easy to forget me? All these thoughts, and what seemed like a hundred more, filled my heart and mind. I just wanted to jump out through the bathroom window, run back to school, and ask Miss Burnell to take me home with her. But then I thought of my brothers and leaving them behind. It wasn't what I dreamed of, or even what I needed, but it was home. I whimpered quietly and then washed my face so it didn't look like I was upset. I took a deep breath and then came out of the bathroom. Old dude was gone, and Mommy looked upset. I forgot about my hurt feelings and decided I had to cheer her up before she got into one of her moods and started drinking again.

"I mem-or-ized a poem and Miss Burnell said me and Pierre are going to say it in front of some school tomorrow. She said she's gonna come pick me up at 6:30pm. You wanna come?" The invitation came out of my mouth before I could take it back.

"Sure, I'll come." She went into the bedroom and left me standing in the kitchen perplexed.

Did she say she was gonna come? I yelled to her, "You sure, Ma? It's gonna be tomorrow, you know?"

"Yeah, I wanna hear your poem."

My God! What was this? This was my opportunity to change our lives! If my mother came to see me do what I did in Miss Burnell's office, I'm sure she would react the same way. She would have no other choice but to be proud of me and love me. She would see that there was no reason for her to drink or to sleep with strange men, and she would never leave us alone, again. We would probably move out of the hellhole we called home and move to co-op city near Titi Ann. Life was going to change, and it was all on me. I had to make it happen.

I know what you're thinking, but cut me some slack; I was eight years old and I had dreams. That was the dream of all dreams. My mother would see how special I was, and our lives would change forever. Unrealistic? Perhaps, but my dream was very real to me, and I was not about to let anyone get in the way of making my dream come true. I was so excited that all I did was practice in front of the mirror in the hallway, until I fell asleep. I went to bed that night and told God about my dream and asked Him to help me make it happen. "Please God.

Please let it happen. Let my mom see the special thing I have so we can get outta here. Thank you for your help. Night."

Thursday was a blur. I remember going to school and maybe playing one game, but I kept pulling Pierre aside to practice the poem with me.

We had it perfected, and I felt confident that we were going to make Miss Burnell proud. At some point that day, Miss Burnell pulled me and Pierre out into the hallway and said "Go!"

I was on it. "I dream a world…"

Pierre did his piece, and she clapped for us and hugged us both. "Pierre, I'm picking you up at 6:00pm, and Dymond, you at 6:30pm. Both of you be ready because we have to be at the school and on stage at 7:15pm."

"We'll be ready, Miss Burnell. Promise." I spoke for Pierre and myself because I had more on the line than he did.

I ran home thinking of nothing but the performance for that night. I wasn't thinking about Julian or anyone else, I was focused and determined that this was the opportunity that was going to change our lives. Julian would probably be nice to me after tonight, knowing that I was the one that saved us. I had one dress. It was forest green with yellow buttons, black tights, and my Buster Brown black shoes that were too small. At lunch time, Miss Burnell asked one of the teachers to comb my hair so I didn't have to do anything with it. I was thankful mommy was home, but her face looked very sad. I decided not to mention it or ask what was wrong. I didn't want to highlight the obvious and have her change her mind about coming. I kept it upbeat.

"Hey, Ma, where's Darrin and Julian?"

"Darrin is 'sleep. Julian is still at school. I guess he should be coming home now."

"Okay, I'm just going to get changed then…in the bathroom."

"Mm hmm, go head."

I went into the room, threw my book bag down, and quietly went over to the crib where my little brother was sleeping on his back. I bent down and looked through the crib bars to make sure his chest was going up and down, and he was breathing. I heard of babies dying in cribs, but no one ever knew how, so I was always checking to see if he was good. He was good. I straightened up and stroked his hair. "Things are gonna get better from tonight on, popi."

I went into the closet and pulled my dress off the hanger. I went over to the dresser and took out the only tights I had, and then went under the crib and got my shoes. I shook them out on my way to the bathroom to make sure there were no roaches in them, and then I got changed quickly. I had outgrown the tights, but they were all I had, so I stretched them as much as I could to make them sort of fit. I brushed up the edges of my hair and looked at myself in the mirror. "Okay, Dymond, this is it. Don't mess up."

I came out of the bathroom and headed back into the bedroom with my school clothes folded, and put them in the dresser drawer. I noticed Darrin wasn't in the crib anymore. I went into the living room and there Darrin was with my mother and Julian. I hadn't even heard him come in. "Hey, y'all. Hi, booboo!" Darrin waddled over to me with his hands waving. I picked him up for a second but then put him down because I didn't want him to mess me up. Julian looked at me, confused.

"Where you goin'?"

"Miss Burnell is coming to pick me up. Me and this kid from my class are gonna perform a poem at a school in front of lots of people."

"Oh yeah? Well good luck, I hope you do good."

I looked at him to see if he was being sincere, and it looked like he was, so I let my guard down for the moment. "Thanks, J, I will." I sat down on the couch and played with Darrin a little bit. Then I brought him into the room and changed his diaper and his clothes. I didn't want Mom to have to do anything, because it looked like she was already stressed out by something. This evening was going to take her mind off of whatever it was that was bothering her. Darrin was ready. I was ready. Julian was still in his school clothes, so everyone was ready to go.

Before I knew it, there was a knock at the door. I carefully sat Darrin down on the couch and ran to answer it. It was Miss Burnell. She actually came. I thought to myself, *She's so brave.* My neighbourhood was full of Black people and Puerto Ricans. Many of them would not have appreciated what Miss Burnell was trying to do for me. They would only see her skin colour and attack her without asking any questions. They had been beaten down so long by white people that they didn't know the difference between the racist ones and the loving ones. For a white lady to be here in the South Bronx, she had to be brave and very determined. She kept her car running and left Pierre there, waiting. She told him to lock the doors until she came back. Then she ran past the rats and into the building, and now she was standing in my doorway, as promised. This was finally happening. My dream.

"Hey, lil Dymond, are you ready?"

"Yes, ma'am, we're ready." I turned and took my jacket off the kitchen chair and saw my mom coming from the living room and heading into the bedroom. "Ma, Miss Burnell is here. You ready?"

"Girl, please, I ain't goin' nowhere witchu." She walked off and closed the bedroom door.

Miss Burnell saw the look of utter shock and rejection on my face and knew exactly what to do. She picked me up and ran back outside, leaving Julian to lock the door. Pierre saw her coming and unlocked the door just in time for her to put me in the backseat of the car, put my seat belt on, and drive off.

Pierre saw my face and was curious and a little concerned. "What happened?"

"Nothing, Pierre, Dymond is fine. Aren't you, honey?" She looked at me through the rearview mirror and continued to say, "You don't worry about anything. You are both going to do just fine."

For a while, no words were able to connect from my heart to my lips, but after two or three minutes into the drive, the reality of the moment began to sink in and it came out with a rage I never experienced before. "I don't care about this stupid poem! I didn't want to do this anyway, this is dumb! I don't care if she doesn't want to come 'cause I didn't want her to come anyway! She would have just brought Darrin and he would have made noise. If she thinks I care, she's wrong. I don't care! I don't care about her, and I don't care about saying this stupid poem. It doesn't even matter." I went on and on, and poor Pierre was becoming more and more confused, especially when he heard me say, "I'm not doing this anymore, you can just take me home. Pierre can do the whole stupid thing."

Miss Burnell kept cool the whole time and just kept on saying the same three things. "It's okay, Dymond. I believe in you. You can do this." Over and over, she just kept on saying this. I couldn't understand why she was so calm about everything. It was almost like she knew something that I didn't.

Pierre tried his best to talk to me, but he was no help. "Shut up, man, you're g'tting' on my nerves.

I'm about to knock you if you don't shut up, man. And you're ugly!"

Pierre couldn't understand why I was attacking him like that when he was just trying to help me feel better. He didn't understand and he would never understand how it felt to have your dream shattered in pieces on the floor for everyone to walk over and ignore. He would never understand the utter worthlessness I felt from that rejection. The pain was too much to put into words, and if it was just one feeling maybe I could have handled it, but it was more than just pain. It was pain, hurt, anguish, worthlessness, anger, confusion, a sense of loss, and deep, deep sorrow.

We got to the school and were brought backstage. Miss Burnell was still saying the same three lines. "It's okay, Dymond. I believe in you. You can do this."

Yo, this is truly getting on my nerves. She saw everything; she must know it's not okay. Why is she saying that, over and over? The last time she said it, she bent down, held my face, and said it while she was looking straight into my eyes. What made her treat me with so much gentleness and patience? I really didn't understand it, but in that moment, with everything I was feeling, I believed her love and care for me. I decided to take the strength and courage she used to come to my hood onstage with me. Miss Burnell never lied to me. She always kept it real, and I could always trust her. Maybe she knew something that I didn't. She knew I could memorize the poem before I knew it. Pierre was pacing and scared that he might have to do it by himself. I peeked out into the audience to see how many people were there. It was like ten thousand! Okay, it was probably a couple hundred, but at eight years old it looked like ten thousand. I looked at Pierre, who looked like he was going to pee his pants. I looked at Miss Burnell, and she asked, "You ready?"

I took a deep breath, grabbed Pierre's hand, and said, "Let's go."

I decided to trust Miss Burnell and follow through on my promise to her. After all, she had gone through so much for me. I owed her. But I wasn't going out happy; I was going out with all kinds of different emotions that I was going to use to perform this poem. I wasn't sure how it was going to sound, but at that point I had nothing to lose.

Pierre and I walked very confidently, almost stomping, onto the stage. Everyone was looking at us, so I also felt nervous on top of the other feelings. I let go of Pierre's hand, took a deep breath, and grabbed the mic like I had something to say. I started to recite my part of the poem like I was the leader of the Black Panther Party. The words were exactly the same as when I practiced, but the sentiment had changed. I felt Pierre looking at me out of the corner of his eye like *"What the heck are you doing? We didn't practice it like this."*

His turn was coming up, and he had to decide how he was going to deliver his portion of the poem. He couldn't look like a punk. He had already heard some of the audience responding to my portion of the piece, saying stuff like, "Amen, go 'head, lil mama." So Pierre decided to follow suit. He changed his stance and went straight BX on them.

When we finished, I felt like someone else. I felt like I was in a dream. It blew me away that the whole auditorium was standing up, cheering and applauding for us. I was in shock and, for the second time that night, I was overwhelmed with emotion, not knowing what to do. It was only when Pierre grabbed my hand and took a bow that I even took in what was really happening. *We killed it!*

We bowed again, and this time I was fully present in the moment. As we walked off the stage, hand in hand, I felt confused. How could I have so much pain and joy at the same time? How could I feel so much worthlessness and accomplishment both at the same time? Miss Burnell grabbed us both and hugged us tightly. "I knew you both could do it. I'm so very proud of you both!" Miss Burnell looked like she had water in her eyes when she held my face in both her hands. "I told you that you could do it. Sometimes we have to climb mountains, lil Dymond, and sometimes we have to go through some valleys, but it's all to make us stronger. Never stop believing in yourself and sharing your special gift, because it's not just for you, it's for others." She hugged me again, and I felt warm in my heart and remembered my dream.

Maybe I was special after all. I knew I had some more mountains and valleys to go through, as Miss Burnell put it, but now I had something that I never knew I had before. I had a gift. It was the thing that made me special, and it wasn't just for me. I was going to offer this gift to others as I grew. It was going to help me through hard times when I needed it to.

"Thank you, Miss Burnell. And thank you, Pierre."

Pierre, overwhelmed with the moment, hugged me and whispered, "I knew you weren't angry at me, but you should know you're real pretty when you're mad."

I smiled as we left.

When I got home, my mother opened the door and didn't even thank Miss Burnell for dropping me off, or taking me, or anything. She just opened the door and walked off, assuming I would lock it behind me. I thought that was so rude, but that was my mother sometimes. Miss Burnell didn't let that faze her at all. "Night, Dymond. I'll see you at school tomorrow. Great job."

"Bye, Miss Burnell, and thank you."

I locked all the locks that were on the door and became very quiet because I knew Darrin was probably asleep. I walked into the bedroom and quietly took off my clothes and put on a ripped t-shirt, shorts, and socks. Mom was lying down on the bed. When I went out to the living room, Julian was watching *Welcome Back, Kotter*. "How was it? Did you do good?"

"Yeah, they stood up and clapped for us." I said it like it was no big deal, because with Julian you just don't know when a fight was going to pop off. His niceness could be a trick to make me think we're cool and then all of a sudden, boom, I get sucker punched.

"That's good. I knew you were mad the way Ma just dropped you like that."

Oh wait, he actually peeped that and cared about how I felt? I was a bit surprised, but kept it in. "Yeah,

I was mad, but I'm good now."

"Yeah right. If I were you, I'd still be mad."

I replied while looking at the television. "Ain't no point in stayin' mad at her, won't change nothing. Plus, I realized that I didn't need her anyway. I did it by myself. I don't need her approval. I don't need nobody." I didn't want to talk about it anymore, so I made myself yawn and said, "I'm tired, man. Goodnight."

Julian watched me walk out of the living room and gave me a look that said, "You ain't foolin me, shorty. I've been where you are. You're still mad."

I got into the bed and didn't even bother saying goodnight to Mommy. Miss Burnell was right, there were going to be a lot of mountains and valleys that I would have to experience. Right at that moment, I was in the valley, and it was really foggy. The tears wouldn't stop flowing, and my pillow caught all of them. I wasn't sure why my mother decided to hurt me so deeply that day, but it was a moment frozen in my mind, and one that I would never forget. My life was full of mountains and valleys alright, and that night was full of the highs and lows of both.

School was my mountain where I would dream, and home was the valley that tried to take those dreams from me. But I found out I was special, and now it was on.

Strengthen the Shell

"Embracing what life throws your way while maintaining your hope and dreams equals resilience." ~Dymond

I woke up the next morning with a harder edge than I had the day before. I was prepared for whatever disappointment came my way. I didn't see my new found perspective as a bad thing; I just saw things more realistically. I looked around the room, and my mother was sleeping. The whole apartment was quiet. I went to the bathroom to wash up and get ready for school. As I looked at myself in the mirror, I saw something different. It was confusing. Because of last night, I knew that I had something special inside me, but a part of me didn't really care. After brushing my teeth and washing my face, I looked at myself for a long time, then finally the words came out.

"No matter what happens today, stay strong and don't cry. That crying stuff is for babies, and this world don't have no room for babies. It's time to grow up now."

I left the bathroom and looked at the clock. It said 8:30a.m. I was surprised Darrin hadn't woken up for his bottle yet. I went over to the crib. He was breathing. I quietly got dressed and went to fix him a bottle. There was no milk in the fridge, and I wasn't surprised. I looked in my mother's purse. There was no money. Again, not surprised. I took a piece of paper from my notebook and folded it up. Then I unlocked all the locks on the door and looked out to make sure there were no drunk people outside on the steps waiting to bother me or grab on me. I went outside and put the paper where the lock was, so I wouldn't get locked out. I ran down the stairs, through the front door, past the rats in and around the garbage can fighting for food, and made a left into the corner store. Julio knew me real well.

"Hey, lil mamita. Buenos dias, como estas?"

"Hey, Julio, buenos dias. Ta bien gracias, y tu?"

Julio was a sweet man who cared about the neighbourhood and the people who lived in it. He knew who my parents were, and he knew how we were living, and I believe he knew what I came in there for. I went down an aisle and quickly put a can of Carnation milk up my shirt. He must have seen something sticking out of my shirt, but he always had pity on me and let me get away with stealing. I didn't do it all the time, just when I needed to, when I had no choice. I ran back past the rats, up the stairs, and was able to get back into the apartment. I was afraid Julian was going to wake up and lock me out. I quietly closed the door so I could keep just a little more peace and quiet before everyone woke up. Then I got a knife and stabbed two holes in opposite ends of the can so it could pour out easily. I washed out the bottle as best I could by pouring soap in the bottle and then shaking it up with hot water. I kept pouring it out and pouring in more hot water until there were no more soap suds. Then I poured in half Carnation milk and half water in the bottle. I shook it up then went into the bedroom. My mother was up, sitting at the edge of the bed, slouched over rubbing her head like she had a headache or something.

"Where were you, Dymond?" She turned around just in time to see me give Darrin the bottle I had prepared. "Where'd you get that?" She knew what wasn't in the fridge.

"I went to the store. Here, popi, drink it." Darrin had his eyes still closed but his hands automatically stretched out for the bottle. He put it right to his head, and I knew it would be done in three minutes flat. That boy didn't play with his bottle.

"I'm going to school. Bye."

My mother jumped up from the edge of the bed. "Wait a minute, no, you're not. I'm walking you."

"If I wait for you to get Darrin ready, I'll be late." I started to walk away while I was still talking, then turned while I was halfway in the hall. "Plus, I walk myself all the time anyway. It's no big deal."

Mom looked at the clock that was at her side of the bed. It was one of those clocks that would allow you to see the numbers flip after sixty seconds. It was also one that had an alarm that my mother never used. "What time is it? 8:50? Why didn't you wake me up?"

She got up from the bed and rubbed her eyes. I was waiting for her to ask me about Julian. She didn't, and I wasn't about to take on the responsibility of getting him up.

"Okay, well have a good day, Dymond."

I rolled my eyes, turned back to grab Darrin's little foot through the crib bars and gave his toes a kiss. "Bye, popi. I'll see you later on, okay? Be good." I turned and walked through the hallway, through the kitchen, picked up my book bag that was sitting on the chair along with my jacket, unlocked the door, and left. I didn't care if the door slammed because Darrin was already up.

I was off to school and determined to make it a good day, regardless of how it started.

When I got to school, I felt the freedom train heading my way. Miss Burnell was greeting all the children as usual. She noticed my mother wasn't with me and my hair wasn't combed thoroughly. "Good morning, Dymond, where's Mom today?"

"Uh, she slept in, and I didn't want to be late." After saying that, I didn't wait for a response, I just put my head down and headed in. Then I heard Miss Burnell clear her throat like she was about to say something else to me, but all that came out was, "Oh okay, Dymond."

I proceeded into the yard and said, "Good Morning, Miss Burnell."

There was no need for me to be cold to Miss Burnell, she was my home girl and someone I could actually trust. The bell rang just as I walked into the yard, so I went to line up.

"Pretty eyes." It came from behind. "Morning, pretty eyes. You were great last night."

"Hey, Pierre, thank you. Yeah, you were sorta fly, too. I never seen that side of you before. It's kinda cute."

Pierre looked at me like I had three heads.

"Kinda? Girl, please, you know I'm fine." I turned and gave him a half smirk and the corner of my eye. Yeah, he was cute, but with all I had learned in the last twenty-four hours about disappointment, I couldn't let him know that. He would just use it against me, and I wasn't having that. If there was one thing I learned, it was to never get caught wearing your heart on your sleeve. This game just went from checkers to chess, literally overnight, and I was going to make sure I was the one saying "Checkmate" when I was ready to make a move. I really didn't want things to be like this, because things actually felt right when he was pursuing me. But something happened to my heart, and I wasn't in control of opening it up anymore. I developed a hard edge that now had a section of my heart walled up, not all the way, but enough for me to keep my composure.

We got into class and took off our coats, changed our shoes, and went to sit down on the carpet. I wanted to sit next to Tatyana to tell her what happened, but the carpet was already packed with kids, and there was no space next to her. She looked back at me. "Come on, come over here." She patted a spot at the edge of the carpet, but then I wouldn't be able to see Miss Williams so I stayed where I was.

I mouthed to her, "I'll talk to you after."

We started the day like we always did, pledging allegiance to the flag of the United States of America, singing how beautiful spacious skies were, and then telling Miss Williams what day it was. We sat down, and Miss Williams started to read a book that I'm sure would have been very interesting if I didn't doze off. I was tired. I had tossed and turned most of the night and then had to get up and take care of business. I loved school, but sometimes I just wasn't altogether there. Sometimes it was because of hunger, sometimes it was because I was angry, and sometimes it was because I was dead tired. I didn't want Miss Williams to call me out, so I put myself behind Geraldo. I knew he liked me and he wouldn't mind me sitting close to him. Plus, he was bigger than me so he could block Miss Williams from seeing me. My elbow, supported by my right knee, in turn supported my right fist, which faithfully supported the right side of my face that agreed with my eyes to take a little break. Just when I was hitting that good sleep, Miss Burnell came into the class.

"Good Morning, class."

I woke up to the chiming of children singing, "Good Morning, Miss Burnell!"

I quickly sat up and wiped the drool that was slowly escaping the right side of my mouth onto my hand. As I sat up at attention, I thought, *How long has she been standing there? Did she see me? Oh man, I hope she didn't see me.* I was oblivious to the fact that Miss Burnell knew all about me and my home life. She knew about my mother being an alcoholic from the liquor she smelled on her breath when she dropped me off sometimes. And she knew that I was lying when she didn't drop me off. She knew my mother was a lady of the night, because one night after working late at the school, she was blocked in by a car that had stopped to talk to a hooker. She beeped at the car to move so she could get out, and my mother, who was high at the time, cursed her out. "Who you beepin' at, honkey? You gonna have to wait...shit! I'm talking, dammit!" She waited and the car moved after my mother got in. She never saw my father, but that was the norm for most of the kids that came to C.E.S. 236—being fatherless. She did see some of the bruises that I had on my arms one day after Julian decided to walk me to school and throw jabs at me all the way there. I never knew that she knew about my struggle, but she did, and her compassion and constant kindness for me had my loyalty forever. She was a hair combing, cookie smuggling principal, but more than that, for me she was a mother figure that God put into my life to keep a small portion of my heart available so that love could access it when the time was right. She just cared with her whole heart and her heart always touched mine.

She had something behind her back that morning that we were all trying to see. "Last night, Dymond and Pierre recited a poem called "I Dream a World" by Langston Hughes himself. They did such an amazing job that everyone stood up and clapped for them. What Dymond and Pierre didn't know is that it was a poetry contest, and they won first prize!" She then took two gold trophies from behind her back and presented them to us. "Congratulations! Dymond, Pierre, come on up and get your trophies."

I was in shock. Was it real? Was this a joke? *For me? Poetry contest? What the...?*

It took me a minute to process what was happening, Miss Burnell had to say, "Come on, Dymond, this is for you."

When I snapped out of it, I quickly got up and pushed people out of the way to get my Oscar...I mean my trophy. Okay, well it felt like an Oscar, I promise you the performance was an Oscar-winning performance, that was for sure.

"I'm coming, Miss Burnell. Move out the way, stupid, coming through. Watch out, man, I gotta get my trophy." I tried to get up to the front of the class quickly, and I wasn't at all sympathetic to the people I had to maneuver through to get there. When I got there and Miss Burnell placed it in my hands, I read my name out loud, "Dymond Avila. Wow, they spelled my name right and everything."

"Yes, congratulations, you did a wonderful job, and we're all proud of you. Everyone let's give them a hand."

The whole class, even Miss Williams, started clapping for me and Pierre. I looked at him and shook his hand. "Congrats?"

"Uh, yeah, yeah...you too."

We both laughed because we really didn't know what to do. I was grateful for Miss Burnell cutting the awkward moment with, "Okay, everyone, carry on with your day."

I started to walk around the crowd of kids to sit at the back, and Miss Williams tried to help as she reached for the trophy. "Here, Dymond and Pierre, I'll put your trophies up on the shelf for you until you go home so nothing happens to them."

I pulled away quickly. "No way! Is you crazy?" It came out so fast I wasn't able to censor it. "I'm sorry, Miss Williams, what I meant to say was nothin's gonna happen to it. I got it. I'll be okay."

Miss Williams had never heard me speak like that before and still had a look of shock and objection on her face as I was apologizing.

Miss Burnell jumped in, "It's okay, let her have it. I'm sure Dymond won't let it come in the way of her school work today, will you?"

I nodded so fast my brain should have been scrambled.

For the rest of the day, I was trying to understand what had happened. *I won something? Me?* I had never won anything in my life. I didn't know how to feel or act. I went through previous night, over and over in my mind, trying to figure out what I did to deserve this.

Tatyana had both hands on both of her cheeks with both of her elbows resting on her desk. I was pacing back and forth, and her eyes were pacing with me.

"I just memorized a poem, Tat. This is crazy!"

"Maybe it was the way you said it, too," She suggested. "You said you were mad that night, right?"

I stopped pacing. "Yeah, I was so pissed, I was seeing red."

Tatyana moved from sitting on the chair and leaning on her desk to sitting on the edge of her desk, listening to my every word.

"I was mad 'cause my mom made me feel like I was nothing, Tat." I looked at her and felt the tears welling up in my eyes, but I refused to let them out. Tat knew me too well, though, so she came over to me and put her arm around me.

"You know how your mom is. I'm sure she didn't mean it."

The tears started to go back into my eyes. "It don't matter now, 'cause I don't care, for real. But Miss Burnell kept on saying that she believed in me and that I could do it. And you know how she looks at you straight in the eye and makes you believe stuff...I believed her."

Tatyana jumped back onto the other desk and started reshaping her afro puffs. "Yeah, girl, Miss Burnell has that look she gives you, and you just gotta do what she asks 'cause you know she's counting on you. I know whatchu mean."

I could talk to Tat about anything. She understood me like no one else. I didn't even have to fully explain stuff, she just got it. "Yeah, girl, it was weird. Pierre was looking at me like I was goin' crazy 'cause I was saying I wasn't gonna do it. Then when I finally decided to do it, I did it different than how we practiced it. I think this way was better 'cause everyone was excited and going crazy for us."

"How did you feel when they were standin' up clappin' for y'all?"

"Honestly and truly, Tat, it's hard to describe 'cause I never felt that feeling before. It was like five feelings all at once."

"Whatchu mean five feelins?"

"I mean I felt happy, angry, excited, mad nervous, and real serious about getting my thoughts out through the poem, all at the same time. It's hard to explain, but when they were clapping for us, I felt like they understood what I was trying to say, like they knew how I was feeling, you know?"

"Wow. Well, I'm happy for you, girl."

"Thanks, Tat."

Tatyana jumped off the desk she was sitting on and hugged me. "I'm real happy that you won that trophy. I'ma get caught up on my script writing before Miss Williams finds out I'm behind, and uh, I see Pierre is sittin' next to your desk now. What's up wit dat?"

"I dunno, but I know I'm not gonna let him know I like him yet."

"Uh, sorry D, I think he already knows that." Tat walked away laughing to herself.

"You think so?" I whispered, then got myself together and walked over to my desk and got started on my work.

The morning flew by, and everyone wanted to touch my trophy. I kept everyone's hands off and held it myself so they could see it and read my name. After lunch, we went outside to play in the playground for some free time. I put my trophy in my cubby, knowing that it would be safe there. Geraldo and Gregory yelled as they were running outside, "Hurry up, Dymond, we 'bout to play tag."

Geraldo and Gregory were two of my friends that I knew liked me, but I was waiting to make my move with Pierre. They wanted to play kissing tag. They usually don't play that game, but that morning I was like a celebrity or something, so now they wanted to play. I didn't care about that. I knew Tatyana loved that game, so I asked Tat and another girl if they wanted to play. Tat said yes way too fast, but the other girl, Cynthia (we called her Cyn), didn't know how to play, so we had to explain it to her.

Tat started, "Okay, Cyn, this is easy. You run and pretend you don't want the boys to catch you, but you really do."

Cyn looked confused. "I do? Why?"

"Because we want them to feel up on our booty, grab us, and kiss us," I chimed in. "Now are you playin' or not?"

You could tell she felt the pressure that Tat and I were putting on her. "Um, okay, I'll try it."

"Cool. Tat, you go that way." I pointed left. "Cyn, you go that way." I pointed towards the right. I'll go down the middle. Let's go."

I never got a lot of attention at home and now I was getting attention from Miss Burnell, my whole class, my friends, and the boy I liked. Shoot, I honestly didn't know how to handle it. There was a part of me that felt alive and special, like I was worth something, like I wasn't an accident or a burden or a mistake. There was a part of me that felt like my dreams just might have a chance and then I would hear a still, small voice say, "*Dream on,*

Dymond." But there was another part of me that was getting stronger since last night. It was a part of me that said, "*Don't feel anything. Hide your heart. Do you. No one cares about you, little girl, so take care of yourself, and most of all...stop dreaming.*"

That part of me was growing without my control, and the thing is I felt like it was necessary for my survival. There was a little fence around my heart that kept me cautious. It was forming a shell that kept me safe, or so I felt. As I ran in the playground looking for Pierre to see if he was going to play with us, I saw him playing with another Puerto Rican girl, Sonia. I ran up to him.

"Yo, you playin?"

"Yo, can't you see we're talkin? Damn!"

I ran off in another direction with the second shock of the day. I didn't know what to say or how to react to that. What happened? Did he think I didn't like him anymore? Why was he treating me like a nobody? I was sure there was an answer, and I was going to get it. He wasn't going to call me 'pretty eyes' in the morning and shoo me off like a fly in the afternoon. *Oh, hell no!* I stopped running, not even concerned about Geraldo or Gregory running up to me and trying to kiss me. I walked back over to him while he was still talking to Sonia and interrupted with attitude. "Pierre, what's your problem?"

He didn't even look up. "Nothin', I'm good."

I persisted. "Nah, you're not good, my brotha, you actin' real dumb right now, and I wanna know who the hell you think you talkin' to?"

He put his head down and didn't say anything, so I continued. "You either tell me right now or when I see your mother today I'm gonna tell her we're boyfriend and girlfriend."

He jumped up before I could finish the sentence, "Okay, okay! Chill!" Pierre looked scared right away. I knew I had pushed the only button that would make him move. He took my hand and pulled me to the outside of the playground to the pavement. "Listen, pretty eyes, Sonia is my cousin, and she just told me that my mother told her mother, which is my aunt, to watch who I play with. My mother knows you, and she said 'cause you're mixed with Black that I'm not allowed to play with you."

I was immediately hurt. "What is your mother's problem? Does she know that I'm Puerto Rican, too? And that we come in all shapes and colours? Ay dio."

He was ashamed, but continued to plead her case. "I know, but she's serious, and Sonia said she has to tell her mother and her mother will tell my mother, so I have to act like we're not friends."

I shook my head "Hold up...Hold up! Who cares if I'm a Black Latina, Pierre? I mean, for real, we're in grade three. It's not like we're gonna get married tomorrow. I just...I just like you, Pierre, that's it. There I said it, you happy now?"

I was really mad at myself for telling him how I felt. It came out unexpectedly. I rolled my eyes and turned my head so he couldn't see my face, but he moved so he could stare right in my eyes. He smiled and looked in my greenish-blue-orange eyes and smiled. "Ha ha, I knew you liked me."

I hated the fact that his laugh had his tongue hanging out like a dog, and he was jumping around like he just conquered something, but he was still so damn cute. "Don't get happy 'cause I don't even like you anymore. I just wanted to find out why you were trippin'."

I turned to walk away from him fast, but he caught my hand while I was walking away and gently whispered, "It's not me, Dymond. I have to do what my mother and father say or I'll get in trouble. But listen, pretty eyes, I like you too, and I want you to be my girl. We just have to keep it a secret."

I couldn't fault him for wanting to get his parents' approval and stay in their good graces. I wanted that same thing. I just knew for me it would never happen. He had a better chance of getting it than I did. I felt the wall coming down as I looked into his eyes. He really meant it. I could tell he really liked me and wanted things to be different. I felt compassion for him and felt myself melting in his smile. Then it happened, again, without warning, a flash of emotion that made me feel like I wasn't good enough. *Be his secret girlfriend? What the heck! Nah, I ain't playin' that game for no one.* I hardened my heart and looked Pierre straight in his eyes. They were begging me to understand and just go along with everything. But instead I said, "Figetchu, Pierre. I never knew you were such a punk. Don't you ever talk to me, again!"

Let's Begin to Build

*"Dreams take on different shapes when
heartache accompanies them...Dream on."*
~Dymond

Pierre was left standing on the pavement with his mouth open. I yanked my hand away from his grasp and walked toward Tatyana, who was hiding from Gregory. Then Miss Williams called us, so we all lined up to go back inside the classroom. Pierre was still trying to get my attention, but he was four people behind me so I acted like I didn't hear anything. Tatyana was standing in front of me and she heard him. Even though she didn't know what had happened, Tat was very protective of me and always had my back.

"Can't you see she ain't talkin to you? Now shut up, stupid!" Tat rolled her eyes and turned around.

"Thanks, Tat, I'll tell you what dat fool said to me later." I didn't bother to look back at Pierre, I didn't want to come across weak, but I was hurt. It was very much like the hurt I had felt the other night with my mom, not as deep, but anything that even came close to that hurt had me running in the other direction.

When we got back into the classroom, it seemed like everyone still wanted to act like we were outside. I felt it for Miss Williams, she had her hands full, but she never looked like she hated us. She always smiled and would call us to the carpet to listen to a book she brought to life that would always calm us down. The rest of the day went by quickly, mostly because I was focused. I couldn't believe I wasn't good enough for Pierre, according to his mom. I mean what was wrong with me? Okay fine, so my hair was a bit confused sometimes—curly one minute and a huge afro the next—but that was only because my mother didn't know how to comb my hair. Was that a reason to treat me like I was nobody? We were just kids, but racist attitudes at any age hurts, and I was definitely hurt. But this time I was not going to be devastated and caught unprepared, I was going to protect myself and my feelings. I was determined not to show Pierre any feelings at all. He wasn't going to get a smile, a smirk, a stolen stare, a brush in the playground, nothing. I would cut him off completely and pretend he didn't exist.

Everyone ran to the carpet to hear a story that Miss Williams had already picked, but I went to my cubby to get my trophy that was still there, safe and sound. I took it and went to find a spot on the carpet to hear the story that I just knew Miss Williams would bring to life. It was like a performance, and I really looked forward to it. I made sure I didn't sit anywhere near Pierre. I found a seat on the carpet next to Tatyana. Through my peripheral vision, I could see Pierre trying to get my attention, but I kept it cool, ignored him, and only talked with the kids around me that wanted to ask me about the trophy and the performance last night. As far as I was concerned, it was *Pierre who?* I could see that he regretted what he had said and the way he treated me, but it was too late. I wasn't about to open my heart to him, again. He finally accepted the fact that I just wasn't going to budge and stopped trying. But I secretly watched him all day and saw that it truly saddened him, and he really didn't know what to do.

At the end of the day, I waited a little while for my mother, but then decided to walk home by myself. I walked through the neighbourhood with so much pride. I still couldn't believe they spelled my name right and that I had actually won a trophy. It still felt like a dream, but a really good one. I started to think maybe there was something to this poetry stuff. The next day I would ask Miss Burnell for some more poetry. I wanted to learn all about it. Maybe I could get good at it. Maybe even learn to write my own. I felt the heart and passion of Langston Hughes' poem, but I had feelings of my own that I could recite. Maybe even scream about. As I got to my door, I quickly put my trophy in my book bag, just in case Julian was home. I didn't want him to touch it. It was the only thing I had that said to the world, "Dymond Avila is special and important!" And I didn't want him messing with it. I closed my bag, and just as I was about to bang on the door, Julian opened it.

"What up, D?" He had a little smirk on his face like he was doing something, so I was on my guard.

"How'd you know I was here?"

"I'm psychic, now come in the house so I can lock the door."

I walked in and locked the door myself while keeping my eye on him from the side, just in case he was luring me in to pounce on me. He seemed cool and just went into the living room.

"Is Mommy home?"

"Does she look home, stupid?"

"I just came through the door, Julian, dats why I'm askin', dang." I quickly went into the bedroom. There was no Mommy and no Darrin. Wherever she was, Darrin had to be with her. I worried about him for a minute but then had to think quickly. My plan was to hide my trophy in my mother's drawer. A place where I knew she would see it but Julian wouldn't dare go. As I went towards the dresser, Julian came running in the room.

"Whatchu doin'?"

"Damn, Julian, are you a ninja or something? I didn't even hear you come in, man. I'm not doin' nothing, just changing my clothes, so if you don't mind, get out."

"You weren't changing no clothes, stupid. I saw you takin' somethin' ouch your bag...lemme see, whatchu got?"

"Nothin, man, I'm tryna change, now get out, J!"

Before I knew it, he grabbed my bag and took out my trophy. "Whatchu doin', man? That's not even yours."

"Oh, this is why you ran in here so fast. Where you get this from?" He stopped to read the trophy and saw that it was from the night before. "First place in a poetry contest? Wow, you something special, Dymond Avila–a-a." He said it like he was announcing something. "I'm proud of you."

I didn't know if he meant it or not, so I didn't respond. "This must mean a lot to you, huh."

"Nah, not really, it's no big deal." My heart was beating so hard I thought he might see it through my shirt. I tried taking deep breaths, but my breathing pattern had changed without me knowing. I was breathing heavy, short, and fast.

"Okay, it doesn't mean anything to you?"

"I didn't say all dat, it's just no big deal, dats all."

"You know what I think…" There was a long pause, and I felt like I was going to have a heart attack. "I think I could take this trophy apart, and you could put it back together."

Oh, Jesus! He's going to destroy it before Mom sees it. How will she know how much she missed? How will she know that I am worthy of her time and attention and that I really am special? I had to think quickly. Maybe I could grab it and run like mad to the bathroom and lock myself in there until she came back. *Is she even coming back tonight?* I didn't know, but I had to try. I kept a calm composure and decided to walk until I got closer to him, then grab it and run. He must have seen the plan forming in my eyes, because by the time I got close he had already determined to keep a firm grip on it. Or maybe I just wasn't as strong as I thought. Either way, when I tried to grab it he was ready.

"Uh uh, I thought you said it was no big deal?"

"It isn't, but I wanted Mommy to see it, dats all."

"She'll see it 'cause you're gonna put it back together."

"I'm not good at dat stuff, J. Just leave it, man." There was too much vulnerability in my tone.

He loved it. He was getting a lot of joy from seeing the terror in my eyes. He was smiling the whole time. He went into the kitchen to get a butter knife to unscrew every screw and pull the trophy apart. He laid it in front of me on the bed. "Don't worry, Dymond, you can put it back together."

Tears filled my eyes for two reasons. Firstly, I was upset my mother wouldn't get to see my accomplishment and see just how special I was. Secondly, I was mad that I still wanted to share it with her, because I still cared what she thought of me when I knew she wasn't even thinking about me. Before I knew it, my trophy, my most prized possession, was in pieces before me, and I had no way of putting it back together. I tried, but it was no use.

Julian left the room. "Good luck, Dymond." I hated him that moment with everything in me. I wished he wasn't my brother. I wished I was in a different family. I wished I was the older sibling. I wished I was braver, stronger. But mostly I wished I had my trophy in one piece. After crying for about five minutes, I ran to the bathroom, locked the door, and cried some more. I talked to God, since I felt like He was my only friend in the world.

"God, why did you let that happen to me? When are you going to help me get stronger so I can fight back?" I didn't hear anything and felt really stupid talking to myself, not to mention weak, because I was sitting there feeling helpless, crying. Then I had a thought. That trophy was special to me, but I had already felt special that night. I started to remember the feeling I felt when everyone stood up and clapped for us. That feeling was still there, I just had to remember it. Even when I felt crushed in that moment by my mother's words of rejection, the feeling of accomplishment, appreciation, and acceptance of my gift was undeniable, and that was what mattered. So feeling crushed by my dismantled trophy was nothing. I had won first place. I was special, and no one in my house knew it but me, and that's just the way it was. I knew it, my schoolmates knew it, Miss Burnell knew it, Miss Williams knew it, and *God, I know you knew it all along. Thank You.*

I determined in my heart that I would continue to grow in performing poetry. I would learn how to write it and get to know as much as I could about other poets and how their writing made a difference in the lives of others. I was going to do the very same thing. Julian didn't know it, but he had done me a favour. My momma didn't know it, but she missed the birth of something great in me.

I got up off the bathroom floor and stood in front of the sink, turned on the water and washed my face. I felt like I got a second wind and knew no matter what happened from here, I was going to be okay. I had hope and a new dream. The dream of my mother coming to see me on stage and loving me had taken new shape. My new dream had me on stage performing in some way, but whether my mom was there or not, I knew I had something great to give to the world, and I was going to do just that, one way or another. Before I left the bathroom, I had to mentally prepare myself to be ready for a fight with Julian. Since my mother hadn't come home with Darrin yet, I knew he would want to torment me some more. I went back on the floor to look under the door on the other side. I didn't see any feet but that didn't mean anything; he could be around the corner, waiting for me. I opened the door quietly and braced myself. No one was there. I stepped out into the hallway and it was clear. I heard the TV going, and it sounded like one of my favorite shows, *Good Times*. I walked out into the kitchen and made a left into the living room. Our living room was huge. We had two couches that faced each other on opposite sides of the room against the wall. One was a pull out couch—Julian's bed—and the other was just for sitting on. Julian was sitting on the couch that pulled out to his bed, so I decided to sit on the other one. He was fully engaged in "Kid Dy-no-mite" so I just thought I'd blend in quietly. Julian didn't miss a beat sometimes, though.

He was still looking at the TV when he said, "Did you do it Dymond? Did you put your precious trophy back together?"

"Yep."

He looked at me in shock. "What? Impossible." He jumped off the couch and ran into the bedroom to see all the pieces still there on the bed. He came running back. "You're such a liar, why'd you say dat?"

"You asked me if I put the trophy back together and I said yes. I didn't say where."

Julian looked at me like I was crazy. "Whatchu talkin' 'bout, Dymond?"

"I put it back together in my mind. It's all in one beautiful piece in my mind."

He looked at me surprised. "Hmm, you not so stupid after all."

In a weird way I took that as a compliment and smiled on the inside.

I got up and went into the kitchen again, this time to see if there was anything to eat. There was nothing but Champale, butter, a half loaf of bread, and mustard. I took a piece of Wonder bread and put mustard on it. I spread it around and pretended that there was bologna, tomato, and lettuce.

"I'm leaving." I grabbed my book bag and my jacket in the bedroom and said, "Later, J."

Julian didn't take me serious, so he didn't bother to respond until after he heard the door slam. By the time I was at the front door of the building I heard him yell, "Where the hell do you think you're goin'?"

"To the library, wanna come?" I knew the answer to that before I even thought up the question.

"You crazy." He sucked his teeth and went back inside the building.

I knew where I wanted to be, and it wasn't in that apartment. I had to get to the library and start to build my understanding of this poetry thing. The library wasn't that close, and I would probably have to answer to an adult if they asked why I was there by myself, but I was willing to figure that out when I got there. I felt like I was just at the beginning of something great, but I had so much to learn.

In the meantime, I had to remember to protect my heart from the hurt that I had experienced from my mother, Pierre, and Julian, all within two days. I had to be smart about who I would open my heart to, because not everyone would know how to handle it. I got to the library after walking for what seemed like forever. It was amazing how differently I was seeing things. I had a new light and a harder edge. I was filled with pain and purpose, ready to take on something new, but not willing to tell anyone about it. It was time for me to go within or else I would surely go without. It was time to cocoon and rebuild.

We Gonna Be Here For A While

"Internal chaos will hush when you embrace the truth about yourself... until then, you fight."
~Dymond

"**D**ymond, come on, man, open the door! Whatchu doin' in there?" Bang! Bang! Bang!

"You're not the only one who needs to use the bathroom, man, open the door." Julian had been banging on the door for at least a half an hour. I didn't care one bit. I was reading some of Zora Neal Hurston's poetry, and I was so captured I didn't even bother answering him. My mother came home and controlled the situation.

"Boy, stop bangin' on the door and come help me with these groceries." Mom was home and she brought food. That was my cue to come out.

My mother was a beautiful woman. She was tall, slender, and always walked like she was on the runway in Paris, modelling some famous designer's clothes. Her skin was flawless, and when she chose to smile, it lit up the room. She loved to sweep her hair up into a French bun; that was her signature look. I ran out of the bathroom with my book and slammed the book on the table when I saw my mother's face. Her hair was pulled back in what I think was supposed to be a ponytail but looked more like a messy tail, she had a track suit on, and no makeup. I had never seen my mother look so tired and worn out before. Something was really wrong. Since Popi had left, Mom had to go on welfare, and we were getting food stamps to get groceries. To me, that was no big deal because it wasn't like we were living in the Hamptons. We were always struggling, so asking for help from the government was no big deal to me, but to my mother it was rock bottom. It hit her pride in a deep way. Sometimes, if Mommy felt really desperate and was feeling for a drink but she didn't have the money, the storeowner would buy her food stamps from her. She would get the money and then buy liquor with it.

Today she had gone shopping, and even though I was shocked by her rough appearance, we were hungry, so I pretended like I didn't notice. I immediately jumped in to help unpack the food.

Julian pushed me out of the way, "Move out the way, stupid." Julian was always trying to control somebody, but this time I pushed back.

"You move out the way, stupid! Ma, what did you get? I'm hungry."

Mom grabbed one of the brown paper bags quickly. "Hold on now! Y'all stop pushing each other. Where's Darrin?"

Is she serious? Why the hell is she asking me about her baby for? Darrin was almost two years old, and I was his mommy every damn day and now she wanted to enquire about how he was doing? *Like really?* I was way too hungry to get mad and say something that might get my face slapped, so I quickly answered her. "He in the crib sleep, Ma. Can I please take the food out?" She let go one of the bags but kept her hand over the other one. Julian and I started taking out the things in the bag we were allowed to look into, and we were naming everything that we pulled out while she watched and smiled.

"Corn Fla-a-akes…a-a-and mi-i-ilk…a-a-and suga-a-ar…a-a-and syru-u-up…a-a-and panca-a-ake…a-a-and be-e-ans…hot do-o-ogs…balogne-e-e…govamint che-e-ese…musta-a-ard…and Wonder bread!"

We were so happy to see the food, but we were more excited to see what was in the other bag, because we knew dinner food must be in there. Julian and I were standing on the kitchen chairs, almost kneeling on the table in anticipation of what we would see next. I wanted to grab the other bag, but Julian was taller and faster, so I let him go for it. Mom was watching us and still held on tightly to the other bag. "Y'all like that? See now I got y'all some stuff, right?"

She was acting weird. I jumped at the bag and grabbed it because she didn't expect that of me, she thought Julian would do that, and I needed to see what was for dinner.

"Wait, Dymond, wait, child… don't grab the bag…"

As I pulled out the first item, ready to sing its name, I quickly said, "Sorry."

The first thing I pulled out was a bottle of vodka. Julian pulled out a case of Champale.

"What the hell? Where's the rest of the food, Ma?"

There were many other bottles of liquor, whiskey,

rum, Colt 45. I was in shock. I couldn't believe it. Did she seriously buy liquor, again, instead of food for us? There wasn't even any baby food for Darrin. I looked my mother right in her eyes. She looked guilty for two seconds and then changed her look to more of a pleading look. "Dymond, the first bag was for y'all and this bag is for me, okay?"

Julian and Mommy were looking at me, waiting for me to respond. I think it was because my face looked crazy. I know this because Julian said, "What's wrong with you, D? Why you look so crazy?"

I was quiet for a minute, then something happened, and I had no control over it. I snapped. I couldn't take it anymore. I jumped off the chair and grabbed the biggest bottle; it was the bottle of Vodka. I ran to the sink and threw it in there. Glass and alcohol went everywhere. It was all in my hair and in the sink and on the floor, but I didn't care. I had enough of her sacrificing our survival for her selfish habit. I didn't think twice about it. I ran back to the table like a mad woman. My eyes were as wide as they could get, and I was breathing heavy and short. It looked like I was about to have an asthma attack, but I didn't care; I had to get the others.

"Dymond, stop!" Mom tried to hold me, but she couldn't. I fought her like I had the strength of ten men.

"No! If we're gonna go hungry, then so are you!"

Julian tried to stop me too, but I pushed him out of the way and grabbed the next bottle. One by one, I smashed every single bottle of liquor that was in that bag, except one. It had already been opened so I opened it up and poured it all out, the whole time looking right at her with an I-dare-you-to-come-

and-take-this-from-me look. Thank God we had one of those deep white cast iron sinks. If we didn't, I'm sure I would have gotten cut way more than I did.

Mom tried to stop me several times. "Dymond, stop…please stop, baby, stop."

I just smashed every bottle, except for that last one that I poured out, in the sink, one right after the other, yelling, "No more! If we don't eat, then neither do you! Enough!"

When I was finished, I certainly looked crazy. My hair was all over the place, my face was red, I was wheezing and breathing heavily, exhausted, more emotionally then physically. I fell to my knees, trying to catch my breath, but I was more overwhelmed than anything. Julian stood there the whole time with his mouth open. He had never seen me that way before. Shoot, I had never seen me that way before. I just couldn't take it anymore, and I was tired of being hungry and uncared for. My mother bent down on the floor with me and tried to console me.

"I'm so sorry, Dymond. I know it's been hard on y'all, too. I promise I'm gonna try to change, okay?"

I looked up with tears streaming down my face and said, "A promise is a comfort to a fool. Keep your promises, Mommy, and just do whatever you want." I got up from the floor and went into my safe spot, yep, the bathroom.

Julian was still standing there, not sure what to say or do. "I'll clean up the sink, Ma. Don't worry, she's just a little upset, she'll be okay."

Mom took Julian's comfort and went to lie down in the room. While I was in the bathroom, I stood on the edge of the tub so I could see myself in the mirror. As I bent over the sink to see my face, I realized there was alcohol and pieces of glass in my hair. My hands had blood all over them because of cuts that I had endured from smashing the bottles. I was still wheezing, but I didn't care. I had reached the end of this drinking journey with my mother, and she had to change or else I would have to start doing something drastic. I looked at myself and said, "You gonna have to grow up even faster, lil girl, life ain't getting any easier." I jumped down, bent over, and shook the glass out of my two wavy ponytails and tried to wash the blood off my hands. I tried to get out as much as I could, but then the room started spinning faster and faster, and before I knew it, I dropped to the ground. I wasn't unconscious; my body had just lost all energy, and it was crashing. I stayed on the floor for what seemed to be hours, but what was really about fifteen minutes. Of course, I woke up to hear Julian banging on the bathroom door and Darrin crying.

"Dymond! Open the door, man, Mom's gone and Darrin's crying. I dunno what to do." Bang! Bang! Bang!

I opened my eyes and actually felt better. I heard Darrin's cry. I shook my head, pushed myself up off the floor, and stood up. After steadying myself, I unlocked and opened the door. I had forgotten that Julian was banging on the door and would be right there to jump me. When I opened the door, Julian was standing there, but he didn't try to knock me out this time. I was so used to getting hit that I automatically flinched and screamed.

"Shut up! Whatchu screamin' for? You need to get Darrin, man. I think his diaper needs to change 'cause it stinks in there."

After I realized he really needed my help, I put my

hands down and went into mommy mode. "So why didn't you change him?"

"I dunno how to do dat stuff...dat's girls' work anyway."

I walked past him, still shocked that he didn't try to hurt me, and went into the bedroom to look after Darrin. Julian went back into the living room. He was right about Darrin, though, it did stink in the bedroom. I immediately went under the crib, grabbed a diaper and the Vaseline, and put them on the bed that was next to the crib. This was where Mommy and I slept whenever she slept at home. "One sec, popi, let me get some toilet paper to wipe your butt." He thought I was gonna take him out, and when I ran back to the bathroom he started to cry louder.

"Dee Dee, Dee Dee, aah aah!"

"I'm comin' back, popi, one sec." I quickly rolled out a lot of toilet paper on my hand and then grabbed a washrag that was hanging off the edge of the tub. I turned on the hot water and soaked the rag then twisted out as much water as my little hands could. I grabbed up the toilet paper and ran back to the room to my crying brother. I put everything on the bed then went over to the crib. The moment I started to walk over there, Darrin started jumping and stretching his hands out to me.

"Dee Dee, up."

"Ok, popi, here we go."

I was a short eight-year-old and always had difficulty getting him out of the crib. He was heavy, and even when I put that side of the crib down, I was still at a height disadvantage.

"Come here, stinky, let's get you cleaned up." I got him out of the crib and laid him on his back on the bed.

He knew the drill with me because he was already saying, "Off." He wanted me to take his diaper off.

"I know, lil popi, let me do it." It wasn't the easiest thing to do because he was always moving. I took the diaper off, and his feet were kicking everywhere. "Listen, keep still." I used the diaper to wipe off as much as I could, then folded it in half and put it to the side. I used the toilet paper to wipe the rest, ripping a piece off at a time till I had nothing left. I put it with the diaper. Then, finally, I used the washrag to get any spots I missed. I plastered the Vaseline all over him quickly before he decided to pee on me. I got the diaper under his butt and the stickers stayed on. The whole time, Darrin was talking whatever language babies talk, and I just kept nodding and saying "Yeah, baby…okay, good boy."

This time around, he behaved himself and there weren't any extra messes. I picked him up off the bed and put him down on the ground so he could walk around and do his thing while I got the diaper and toilet paper off the bed and into the garbage. Darrin headed straight for the kitchen, and I followed. I threw everything out into the garbage in the kitchen and realized I had to make a bottle for him. Julian was watching TV when I asked him where Mommy went. I honestly didn't care where she was at that point. I was still mad at her for putting her needs before ours.

"Where she go, J?"

"Wherever she went, D. Who cares?" This was one of the very few times Julian and I actually agreed on something. I started to make a bottle for Darrin, who kept on running from the kitchen to the hallway closet. He loved doing that because there was a full length mirror on the hallway closet door, and he always thought he had another friend to talk to. He would look at himself, crack a joke with himself, laugh, and run back into the kitchen to hit the fridge like he was playing tag, and then go back to the mirror to do it all over again. Darrin was content in his own little world and oblivious to the life our mother lived. He got fed, changed, loved on, and taken care of. Sometimes I wished I had his life. I put the bottle in the pot of boiling water that was now boiling on the stove, and I knew it would only take a few minutes before the milk was warm. I heard *"Welcome back, welcome back, well we tease him a lot. Welcome back, welcome back, welcome back 'cause we got him on the spot..."* Julian was watching one of my favourite TV shows, *Welcome Back, Kotter*, when Mommy came back.

"Whatch y'all doin?"

I didn't answer, and that wasn't like me. I was never disrespectful or disobedient. I had become a mommy pleaser, but at that moment, the last thing I wanted to do was please her. That hard edge inside me had taken over more than I had realized. And whether she approved of me or not wasn't as important as it was before, my focus was getting my baby brother his bottle. I turned off the stove, got the bottle out, shook it up, and tested it myself. "Come here, speedy, stop runnin' back and forth and drink this bottle, little boy." I caught him on his way back to tag the fridge.

He was smiling and laughing and ready to go again. I picked him up and went straight to the couch in the living room to lay him down so he could hold his bottle and feed. I propped a cushion behind Darrin's head so he wasn't completely flat on his back and so he could drink at a good pace without choking. Mommy came into the living room and sat down next to Darrin and looked at me.

"You okay, Dymond, or you still mad at me?"

I didn't answer. I went to sit on the floor to watch TV with Julian, who had not even acknowledged her presence. I felt a little bad for not talking to her, because I still didn't want to hurt her feelings, even though I knew she didn't care about mine. But I had decided that I wouldn't be like her, and I was going to make sure of that as I grew up.

Mommy was determined to talk to us and didn't take lightly to disrespect. So she went over to the TV, turned it off, put her right hand on her hip as she slightly leaned more on her right knee, and said, "That will be the last time either one of you ignore me. Now get your narrow behinds up on that couch so I can tell you the good news."

Julian and I looked at each other to see who was going to move first. Mommy didn't have patience, so she helped us with a firm grab on our arms. She picked us up off the floor and pushed us onto the couch. Julian and I were bumping into each other on the couch and trying to get comfortable when she started. "Listen, guys, I know y'all are mad at me for buying all those drinks, but believe me, when I went to the store I wasn't even thinking about that. It just happened, sorta. Anyway, that doesn't matter anymore. I have something to ask you both, and I want you to tell me what you honestly think."

We both sat there, looking at her with a blank expression on our faces. "What do you think about moving to Toronto, Canada?"

Part 4

"Break Out, Breathe, & Fly"

Where Am I?

*"Destiny is never in jeopardy of changing, but
some choices can make us detour. Not to worry,
Providence will always step in." ~Dymond*

"Cana-what?" What the heck was she
talking about? I had to look into her
eyes for a long time to make sure she
wasn't high or drunk. She looked crazy, but it looked
like she was actually sober. Julian and I looked at
each other, confused.

"It's not Cana-what, it's Ca-na-da. It's another
country. I have family there, and life is better there,
cleaner, and more quiet." Her eyes gazed off for a
second, like she was remembering something, and
then quickly came back to us. "We could have a
better life there, guys, and leave all of this behind,
you know?"

*What was she talking about? Maybe she was
high. Why did she think we would want to leave our
friends behind?*

"Whoa, whoa, whoa...leave all this behind?
Whatchu talkin' 'bout, Ma?" I had to ask because
she was talking all kind of crazy.

"I'm talkin' about leaving behind this rat-,

roach-, water-bug-infested apartment. I'm talkin' about leaving behind the drinking and partying with people that don't care about me." She got up from her squatted position and started to pace back and forth while she gave us her reasons for why we should take everything we had and move to a foreign country.

"I'm talkin' about leaving all the people behind that did us dirty, Dymond. I'm talkin' about starting over."

We were watching her rant and pace back and forth like a ball in a tennis match. She stopped pacing and came back to the couch, where we were sitting. She squatted to look us in the eyes and said, "I'm talking about a fresh start. We're moving to Canada, and we're leaving tonight."

"What? Hold up, you can't just take us out of school like that!"

"Yes, I can."

"What about our friends?" I asked.

"What friends? We don't got no friends." She answered.

"Rafael's our friend. Tatyana's my friend. Miss Burnell is my friend! I'm not leaving here to go to some crazy country!" Now I started pacing. I looked back at Julian for help. For some reason I felt like we were in this together.

To my surprise, he actually agreed with me. He came and stood beside me. "Yeah, we ain't goin' to some crazy country where we don't even know nobody!"

Mom looked at us and then laughed. "Okay, so now y'all wanna act like best friends, any other time y'all are at each other's throats. We are moving to Ca-na-da, and we're leaving tonight, whether you like it or not. Just know that I'm doing this for us."

I couldn't believe she was saying this. It couldn't be true. I mean, I prayed we would get out of this hellhole, even dreamed about it, but not like this. I didn't know anything about Canada, this wasn't like my dream. It wasn't supposed to happen like this. Julian seemed unusually quiet. I expected him to have a lot more to say, but I was the one freaking out. He just kept on repeating what I was saying, which was annoying.

"You just want to start fresh for you, you're not thinkin' about us! You *never* think about us!" I continued to yell and follow her into the bedroom.

I couldn't understand why my dream of getting out of the hood was going to come true but not in the way I imagined. Could dreams change like that without warning? I wasn't ready, and now we were leaving. Just like that. I didn't have a chance to think. *Leaving tonight? Leaving everything behind?* I wouldn't have Rafael or anyone to have my back or to run to. I wouldn't have Tatyana to talk to, or Miss Burnell to help me with this poetry stuff that I wanted to know more about. I was scared and angry at Mommy for making this decision so impulsively, yet a small part of me started to think maybe this was what it was going to take for her to change her life and our lives for the better. A small part of me thought maybe, just maybe, things were going to be better.

Mommy looked at me with understanding in her eyes. "I know this is a lot to swallow, Dymond, but there's nothing left for us here. I've tried to change my life so many times, and it hasn't worked here. I need to go to a place where no one knows me, where no one knows who I've become or what I do…did.

If there is any chance for me to change my life and give you kids a better childhood, this is it, and I'm gonna take it. The way you children are growing up is just wrong, Dymond. You've seen way too many adult situations. You both have grown-up attitudes, and you haven't really had a chance to just play like I did as a child. There is a simpler way of living, and I want to give that to you and your brothers before it's too late. I know it's hard to understand right now, baby girl, 'cause you're young, but you'll thank me later. Now I'm gonna take the rent money, and we're gonna pack our two suitcases, and we're gonna leave tonight. It's like an adventure. Julian, come here, it's gonna be okay. You, me, lil Darrin, and Dymond are all gonna be alright. Y'all gotta trust me, okay? Now, let's go pack."

We were packed a lot quicker than I thought we would be. I looked around the apartment and she was just rushing, like she couldn't wait to just get out of there. It was winter, so it was cold outside. She told us to get our coats on.

I was confused. "I thought you said tonight, like later on."

"I know, but I changed my mind. Get your jacket 'cause the cab is outside, waiting."

Why was she continually saying shocking things? First it's 'we're moving to a foreign country,' and then it's 'the cab is outside.' I ran to the door, unlocked all the locks, and went across the hall to bang on Rafael's door. "Rafael! Rafael! Please open the door. Ple-e-ease! We're leaving and I have to hug you and tell you how much I love you 'cause I don't know if I'll ever see you again."

The door opened, but it wasn't Rafael. It was Lisa, his girl. She was straight up and to the point, I could tell she really didn't want to open the door, but she didn't want to hear me banging and screaming anymore either. "He ain't here, Dymond. He'll be back in an hour or so."

She was about to close the door in my face, but I started up again. "That's gonna be too late. We're leavin' right now! Oh man, are you sure he won't come back sooner? Is he on the corner or something?"

"No, mamita, he's out with his friends. Where y'all goin'?"

"My mother is makin' us move to another country— Cana-something—and I didn't want to leave without telling him bye."

Mom came outside with Julian and Darrin. Julian was struggling to pull one of the suitcases that was half his size. Mom had Darrin in one hand along with her pocketbook and my coat. The other suitcase was in the other hand. She walked by me and Lisa, struggling with everything, trying to get down the stairs and out the door.

"Come on, Dymond, the cab is waitin', and he ain't gonna wait forever. We gotta go." She handed me my coat.

Did she get a chance to say bye to Rafael earlier? How could she just leave like that without saying anything to anybody? I could see she was on a mission, and there was no stopping her. As I put on my coat and started to walk toward the stairs, I stopped and looked inside the apartment that we were leaving. Mom didn't even bother closing the door. It looked lonely, and I didn't have time to go back and make sure we weren't forgetting anything. As I turned and headed towards the stairs, I screamed out to Lisa who looked very confused. "Please tell

Rafael that I'm sorry I couldn't say goodbye 'cause I had to go quick. Tell him he was the best neighbour. No the best friend and protector and I love him, and I'm gonna miss him."

Lisa nodded to everything I said, but I didn't know how much she was actually going to remember. When I got to the door of our building, there was a big lump in my throat. I was leaving behind all I knew, my whole world was changing, and I didn't know what to expect. School, friends, where were we going to live? How were we going to live? Did Mom have a job? I had so many questions and not enough answers. Julian was helping Mom put the suitcases in the trunk of the taxi.

"Dymond, come on, man! Mommy said we gotta go."

Since when did he become so obedient? This was one time when I needed him to act up, but he was behaving himself like a perfect angel.

"Ma, we have to say goodbye to Rafael. Can't we wait a few more minutes?"

Mommy was so focused on leaving and getting us all in that cab that I don't think she even heard me. The lump in my throat was beginning to hurt, and it was becoming hard for me to breathe. I was walking slowly toward the cab, hoping Rafael would come just in time, but he didn't. Mom didn't have time for me to play around so she put Julian and Darrin in the back of the cab and then came for me.

"Come on, baby girl, it's gonna be okay." She grabbed my hand and dragged me to the cab. She motioned to the back seat as her hand led me to the seat and closed the door. She got into the front seat, and we started to drive off.

I turned around to look out the back window, and

just as we were getting to the bottom of Topping Avenue, I saw Rafael coming towards the building. "There he is! There he is, Mom! There's Rafael! We gotta go back to say bye to him. Hey, mister, turn the car around, I gotta say bye to my friend." He wasn't listening to me. "Hey, did you hear what I said, man? Turn around."

Before I knew it, the lump in my throat turned into uncontrollable tears. We weren't turning around. Mom told him, "Keep going, we have a train to catch." She turned to look at me. "We can't, Dymond, we just can't. I know Rafael's been good to us, and we can write him when we get to where we're going, but we can't go back. We can never go back."

I sat back in my seat and hugged Darrin. He was looking at me confused because he wasn't used to seeing me cry. "Dee Dee...no cry...no cry." He tried to wipe the tears from my face, but I kept my face down and kept hugging him tightly, thinking to myself that this was the end of everything I knew to be real. I would have no protection and nowhere to go if my mother didn't really make a serious change. I felt so alone, so afraid, but there was one thing that I knew I was bringing with me—my dreams and my new found love for poetry. My dreams had taken on a different shape without warning, but I was determined to work with them the best way I could to make sure they still came true. I put Darrin down and told him, "I'm okay, popi. I had something in my eye."

Julian was quiet to the point where I was concerned. He was staring out the window and had said nothing since we left. I didn't know what was going through his head, but I was too busy making sure my tears would stop. I had to get it together. The hardened part of my heart was well acquainted with being tough and strong, so I tapped into that and the lump disappeared. We got to the Grand Central Station in downtown Manhattan faster than I wanted. We got checked in and were seated on the train. This was really happening. Not being able to say goodbye to the people that mattered to me hurt, but the pain made me stronger and harder. Now I was cold enough to guarantee that I wouldn't open up to anyone else. I'd had enough hurt and pain in my life. Having the only people that I loved and trusted ripped away from me was enough for me to shut down my heart completely. Our seats on the train allowed us to look at one another. There was a little table in front of us and Mommy put Darrin's diaper bag on that. It was about 10:30p.m., and we were hungry and tired. The conductor came by and asked for our tickets. Mommy showed him our tickets.

I asked him, "How long is it gonna take to get to Canada?"

He said, "Twelve hours."

I couldn't believe it. "Twelve hours? That's half a day." I looked at my mother. She looked calm,

"Fall asleep, Dymond baby, by the time you wake up we'll be there."

Is she crazy? How am I supposed to sleep after all that drama? I was wired, pissed, confused, scared, and had no idea what was going to happen. Then, out of nowhere, she went into Darrin's baby bag and took out two McDonald's bags. *No way!*

"I know y'all must be hungry," she said. "Eat up and then get some rest." She took a bottle out of the bag, too. She picked up Darrin, cradled him, and started to feed him. I hadn't seen her do that in so long I didn't know what to do. I was shocked that she prepared a bottle for the trip. Shocked that she still knew how to feed him. And shocked that she still wanted to. I stared at them for what seemed to be a long time.

I was brought back to reality when Julian said, "You don't want your food? I'll eat it."

I grabbed my bag of food and said, "Boy, is you crazy?"

I couldn't believe she thought about everything. She planned this whole thing. I ate the burger and fries that were now cold, but I didn't care. *Whatever is waiting for us at the end of this train ride better be good 'cause we're going to be there for a while,* I thought to myself.

Life Changed

"New beginnings are not always easy and don't always come with comfort, but they will always be better than what was. Embrace them."
~Dymond

Canada was nothing like I had ever dreamed. I knew nothing of people saying "Good morning" with no intention of jumping me. The way they talked was weird, but they said that about the way I talked, too. We stayed with Mommy's old friend, whom she knew from her childhood. She lived in Toronto. We stayed with her until we got on the welfare system and got a place of our own. One thing that was apparent to me was that the hood was not just in the Bronx. I was shocked to see that they had poor Black people over here, too. I thought poor Black people only lived in New York City. We stayed in an apartment that was cleaner and seemed peaceful. It was in a place called Parkdale, but we didn't stay there long. Mommy said, "Drug addicts are drug addicts and I don't want nothing to do with them." I knew she was talking about Popi. He had hurt her badly, so I said nothing. I just listened to her as she rambled on about why we moved to Canada in the first place…

blah blah blah.

We moved from Parkdale to another hood that was called Jungle. I was amazed by all the trees and parks. I felt like it was paradise and that Mommy was right—it was a place where we could start fresh. I started to dream again, and even though I missed what I knew because of the people I knew, I was open to making new friends and meeting people like Miss Burnell and Rafael. Since this was the hood too, they had to have a couple of those kinds of people, right?

Before we left Parkdale, Mommy hooked up with a Jamaican family that would later become a second family to me. They connected us to church and invited us to a prayer meeting. Mommy accepted the invitation but had no intention of going, because even though she was trying to do things differently, she still seemed lost. She didn't realize that the feeling of being lost had nothing to do with her surroundings but had everything to do with what was happening in her head and heart. Her dreams of marrying Popi had been shattered and the pieces were scattered in too many directions for her to try to put them back together. So instead, she moved, hoping to find some peace within her shattered heart and maybe another man to fill the void. That said, she had no intention of going to church or getting close to God. That's how she met Popi, and she was not going to get caught slipping, again.

I, on the other hand, was convinced we were going to go to church and was glad we were getting back to God. It had been a while since we went to church and that was one of the places where I would always feel safe and find a sense of peace in the madness of my world. I got Darrin ready for the prayer meeting so we could go when the time came. Julian was out running the streets somewhere. He didn't like Toronto much and would act out as much as he could, thinking that if he was bad enough Mommy would just bring us back to the Bronx. He didn't know that Mom was a Canadian citizen all those years, living in New York, and that she couldn't be deported out of the country. I didn't know that either, but I really wanted to give Toronto a try.

Mommy hadn't given up drinking or partying, but she had started to stay home more and was trying to act like a caring parent. That gave me hope…just a little. I had prayed for this, and even though it was happening slowly, I still believed things were going to get better. "Ok, Ma, me and Darrin are ready to go."

She was sitting down on the couch looking at the TV. "Ready for what?" She didn't even look at us.

"The prayer meeting. Remember that lady invited us?"

"Child, I ain't goin' to no prayer meeting. I just said that so she would stop askin' me."

I was so disappointed. Mommy looked over at us standing at the door, dressed and ready. "Dymond, I'm just tired of tryin' God and failin' all the damn time."

"You won't fail this time, Ma. I know it. Let's go, come on."

She looked at me with pity, almost like she felt sorry for me. "Whatchu think is gonna happen, huh? You think if I go to this prayer meeting I'll stop drinkin' and wilin' out? Is that whatchu think, lil girl?"

I looked my mother in the eye. I don't know how I knew, but I just knew this was her chance to get it right. I really believed if she went to this prayer meeting she would serve God for real this time and stay sober. I hoped for it, prayed for it, and today, somehow, I just knew it. "Yes, I believe if we go to this prayer meeting you will not fail God like that again. Just trust me, let's go."

Mommy squatted her slim frame down in front of me to look me right in my eye. "Okay, Dymond, I'm gonna go. But I'm goin' on your faith."

I was cool with that.

We got there and people were already singing songs. Some of them I knew, some of them I didn't, but I still tried to pick up the words and melody. I was sitting down on the couch directly opposite my mother, who was sitting on a love seat looking like she didn't want to be there. She looked guilty like she did something wrong. She kept her head down. Then everyone started to sing a song I knew.

"I don't know why Jesus loves me, I don't know why He cares, I don't know why He sacrificed His life, oh but I'm glad, I'm glad He did."

After singing the song and believing the words, I started praying really hard for my mother. "God, please, please help her get saved so she can live for you and stop drinkin' and goin' out with all kinda crazy men. Please save her!"

Darrin kept on trying to talk to me. "Dee Dee, wha momma doin'?"

"Shh, just copy me, popi, and pray for momma." He always listened to me, so he did. He clasped his hands together and prayed. I didn't know what he was saying, only God knew because Darrin had such a heavy lisp and he was just learning how to talk. Just then, I looked over and saw Mommy looking over her shoulder like she was looking for somebody. The look on her face went from guilty to scared senseless. I went back to praying and hoping that things would change. I looked at her again and she looked over her shoulder again like she was looking for someone. *Is she goin' crazy, Jesus? All those nights of drinking and tricking and drugs, are they catching up with her?*

The next thing I knew, Mommy fell on her knees and was crying out to God. "I surrender, okay? I surrender. Have mercy on me, Lord. Please have mercy!"

I didn't understand what happened that night until much later, but that night I witnessed a miracle with my own eyes. From that day onwards, my mother never touched another sip of liquor or had another gentleman friend come by, and she stopped going to parties. Instead, she started going to church every Sunday, and she stayed home and cooked for us, helped us with homework as much as she could, and dedicated the rest of her life to serving God. It was a miracle. Mommy had changed, and somehow I knew it would happen. I dreamed it would happen one day, but when it actually did I really didn't know how to act around her.

We went back to our apartment after the prayer meeting. "You okay, Ma?" She was unusually quiet. "I went on your faith, Dymond, and you were right. God spoke to me. I heard Him loud and clear, and my life has changed. We're going to church with them this Sunday."

I was overjoyed that we were going to start going to church. I didn't know what kind of church we were going to, but I just couldn't wait to be there. There was something about the house of God that always brought me peace, gave me strength, and allowed me to dream even more than I normally did. My most creative dreams were inspired by a good message from the pastor. When we got back to the apartment, Julian was sitting in front of the door. We didn't know how long he had been sitting there, but he looked like he had been in some mischief. Mommy looked at him and extended her hand to help him up. "Come on, Julian, let's get you inside and get you something to eat."

I looked at my mother and wondered what she was going to do to him when she got him inside. I just knew he was going to get it. He didn't come home after school and now it was almost eleven o'clock at night. We didn't know where he was or what he was doing. Julian looked at her suspiciously, too. When she extended her hand, he flinched, expecting a slap. When he didn't feel the slap, he looked up and reluctantly took her hand. "Yeah, I'm hungry, but…um…you okay, Ma?"

"I'm great, Julian. Things are gonna change around here, and you don't have to keep on misbehavin' anymore. I know you don't like this place, but we're going to be here for a while so we have to make the best of it, okay?"

Julian didn't say much when we were leaving because he was in shock, but since we moved to Canada he had a whole lot to say. I had never seen him be disrespectful to Mommy before; mischievous, yes, but disrespectful, absolutely not. He was afraid of her, and when she was around he always behaved himself.

"I ain't gonna be here for a little while. I'm leaving." He snatched his hand away from her and looked at her with anger. "If you wanna stay here for a while, that's you. I'm goin' back to the Bronx. I hate it here!"

Mom was unusually calm, to the point of being creepy scary. She was calm like the psychos in those scary movies who were calm just before they lost it and killed everybody. I took Darrin's hand, brought him to the room, and put him to bed, just in case something was to pop off between Julian and Mom. By the time I came out, she had made franks and beans and asked me if I wanted some. Julian was still going off. He was trying to convince her why we needed to leave Toronto and go back to the Bronx.

I walked toward the table and sat down. "Yes, ma'am, I'm hungry."

Mom put the food in front of me with a smile. "I'll get you some juice. Come on, Julian, come and eat something."

I was nervous. I didn't know this mother. *Can someone change just like that? Where did the real mommy go? Why isn't she getting mad at Julian and knocking him out?*

"I don't want no food. I don't want to stay in this stupid place. I want to go home!" Mom put his food down on the table and said, "This is home, Julian. I know you don't like it now, but you'll make new friends, you just gotta give it a chance, that's all."

"I ain't givin nothin a chance. I don't want no new friends, I want my old friends."

"You want the rats and roaches too." I chimed in. "We haven't seen one roach since we been here and this place has so many parks. Come on, J, give it a chance."

"No! I don't care 'bout all that. I don't like it here, and I don't wanna be here! I don't care about y'all, I'll get there by myself!" Julian stomped towards the door. We didn't expect him to actually leave. But he did.

Mommy ran to the door, but she was too late. "Julian, get back here, boy! It's too late for you to be runnin' these streets."

Julian was fast, and before she could finish her sentence he was already down two flights of stairs. She came back into the apartment with a look of concern, and then she did something that I'd never seen her do. She went over to the window and bowed her head and prayed. She prayed for Julian to come back safely! It was then that I realized something different had indeed happened to her. She was serious about trusting God this time, and for some strange reason, I felt like things might just get better. I finished my food and went to bed.

Around 3:30a.m., the police knocked on our door. I ran to the bedroom door to look down the hall and see if maybe it was J. I was wiping the sleep from my eyes when I saw that Mommy still had her clothes on. It looked like she had been pacing up and down the hallway praying for Julian all night, because she had the olive oil out and her hands were glistening. She opened the door and saw Julian with the officers.

"Oh, thank you, Jesus. Are you okay?" She hugged him and kissed his face in a way that I'd never seen before.

I decided to come out of the room to find out what was going on. "Hey, J, you okay?"

Julian pushed Mommy away and wiped off his face where she kissed him. He looked at me as I was walking down the hall toward him and gave me a one head nod. "Hey, D."

The police officers were still standing outside the door. "May we come in, ma'am?"

Mommy opened the door wider for them to come

through as she watched Julian wipe off his face and plop himself down on the couch. "Yes, yes, of course. I'm sorry, please come in. Thank you for finding my son and bringing him home safe. I was worried sick, and I didn't know where to look. I went everywhere I thought he might be and couldn't find him." She was looking at Julian the whole time she was talking with the officers. It was almost like she was trying to talk to Julian indirectly. I came out of my room and headed over to the couch to sit beside him. Normally, I keep far away from him, but with the police there I felt a sudden urge to be his back up. Even though I hated Julian sometimes, he was still my brother and my family.

Mom caught herself staring at Julian and quickly gave the officers eye contact, realizing that they were standing there listening and staring at her waiting for her to finish her ramblings.

"Can I get you some water or tea?"

The officers took their police hats off and stayed close to the door. They were both at least 6' 2" and looked like they worked out on a regular basis. One of the officers was white and the other was black. I thought that was an interesting combination and wondered, for a quick minute, how they actually got along. "No, thank you, ma'am. We wanted to speak to you about your son and what he's been up to. We were called by the superintendent when he heard someone banging on the walls in the laundry room. When he went to check on it, he saw your son with a pipe, destroying the walls in the laundry room. He also saw that there was a small fire that had been started with newspaper. The super grabbed him and called us. There are about ten or more holes in the walls, and a few of the washing machines have been damaged."

Mommy looked shocked by what the officers said. She stood there with her eyes bulging and her mouth wide open. Then she shot a look of disbelief to Julian, covered her mouth with her right hand, and looked back to the officers. After hearing all they had to say, Mommy snapped out of the shock and shouted, "What? Julian, what the hell were you thinking, boy? Why'd you do this?"

Julian looked at her from the corner of his left eye, and I swear he looked like he wanted to kill her. "I… want…to…go…home!"

The officers continued to address my mother. "The damages range between two to three thousand dollars roughly, give or take a few hundred, and the superintendent wanted us to come up here and talk to you about it."

Mommy's face went white. Her beautiful caramel complexion went pale, and she looked like she was losing her balance. "I need to sit down for a minute. Two to three thousand dollars? Officers, I don't have one thousand…where am I gonna…what am I gonna…this is crazy!" She was stuttering and looked obviously confused.

"Were you aware of his whereabouts?"

"Huh? Oh no, he left here upset and I tried to run after him but he's just faster than me. He's having a hard time adjusting to the culture here. We just moved here from New York City, and he had to leave all his friends behind. He hates me for it. I keep tellin' him he'll make new friends, but he's having a hard time believing that. I thought he just needed some space and then he would come back. I didn't think he would cause any damage. This is the first time he's acted this way."

"This is the first time you made me live here," Julian mumbled. "I wanna go home...I hate this stupid place."

Mommy heard the word stupid and shot him a look that assured him she would most definitely knock him out regardless of the police officers. "Whatchu say, Julian? Who you callin stupid, boy? It is way too late. It's the middle of the night, and these police officers just said you tried to set this building on fire, so you know what you need to do—shut up!"

Julian sat there without responding. The police officers watched the interactions and saw, just by the look of our apartment, that what my mother had said was true. We hardly had furniture. There weren't even any pictures on the walls yet. We hadn't been there long enough to set strong roots. We were still getting settled and not sure what to expect.

The police officers looked like they were about to leave. "Listen, ma'am, we'll try to talk to the superintendent on your behalf, we can see you're still trying to get settled here. I'm sure this building has insurance for things like this, but you have a bigger problem on your hands." They walked toward the door. The Black police officer lowered his voice and spoke to my mother so only she could hear him. "If you don't get someone to help you mentor your son, next time he gets angry, because of this new situation that he feels thrown into, he might just succeed and hurt himself or someone else. Please give us a call if you need help in finding a male mentor. We work with Big Brothers, Big Sisters all the time. Good luck."

I wondered why the white police officer didn't say a word. He let the Black officer do all the talking. Maybe that's what they were taught—Caucasian police officers deal with the Caucasian families and Black officers deal with the Black families. Whatever their procedure was, I was glad because I was scared of white people, except for Miss Burnell and Miss Williams, they were cool white people.

Mom thanked the officers again and quietly closed the door. She turned to us, looking lost and disappointed. She walked over to the kitchen table and sat down in a way that clearly showed she was exhausted. She was a very classy lady at all times, even when she sat down, but not this time. She fell into the seat and immediately bent over and rested her elbows on her knees. Her head fell down and, honestly, I thought she was going to pray or cry or something. Her hands held her face as she began to sob. I got real nervous and looked at Julian, who looked emotionless. *What happened to him out there?*

He had that hard-hearted look that I had in the Bronx when I decided to harden up a piece of my heart and feel nothing. Mommy started to talk to Julian through her tears.

"I don't know what to do with you, Julian. I'm lost here, too. It's not just you, ya know. I am trying to give you children a better life! Can't you see that?" She looked up at him with tears streaming down her face. "Don't you see that we can live better over here? Look, look outside!" She went over to the window and pulled back the peach chiffon curtains to show us the big, beautiful neighbourhood. "Look, there are parks that are safe for you to go to, and Dymond can go out and play without me even watching her every minute. It's safe here, cleaner, and even the people are nicer here. Haven't you made new friends at school?"

"No!" Julian stood up and decided he was going to tell her exactly how he felt, regardless of her tears. "No, I haven't made new friends, you know why? 'Cause I don't want no new friends! I want my old friends. I want to walk to the corner store and holla at Keith to come wit me. I want to buy Now & Later candy, but I can't 'cause they don't git that down here. I hate it here. I wanna go back to my hood. Can you understand that, *Jocelyn*?"

I had never heard Julian speak to my mother that way, and I sure never heard him call her by her first name. I was actually scared of what was going to happen next. Mommy's face looked hurt, and it was obvious she would never be vulnerable with him like that, again. She came real close to him, and I swore he was going to get a serious butt whooping, but something else happened instead. I wish I understood then what I know now. Maybe I would have said something or tried to do something, but I didn't know it was as serious as it was for Mommy. She wiped her tears and got right in his face so he could hear her quiet, shaky, hurt voice. "We ain't goin' nowhere, Julian. I'm a Canadian citizen, so they can't deport me back to the States. So you can misbehave at school, and they can call me, but we ain't goin' back. You can runaway, and I'll run right behind you until I find you, but we ain't goin' back. You can even try to set this building on fire with your family in it, but we ain't goin' back! You can try to stress me out all you want, I'ma pray for you, my son. I know how you feel, but we ain't goin' back. So make yourself at home, Julian…'cause our life has changed."

Him

"When REAL love begins you're never ready.
It surprises you, sets you free, and opens up a
different world where two different souls unite
and then..." ~Dymond

Living in Canada was a hard adjustment. It's not that Julian couldn't adjust, he was definitely smart. He just didn't want to. He continued to give Mom grief. Skipping school, getting into fights, and whenever he was at school he was arguing with teachers, or feeling up girls in the washroom, or damaging property. You name it, Julian tried to do it, just to drive my mother crazy. Eventually, he succeeded, because one day I heard her say to herself in the kitchen that she couldn't take it anymore. She said, "No more police are coming to this door. Period."

The Young Offenders Act had many laws that protected Julian, so even when he broke the law and got caught it was just another wasted day in court, because the judge would just slap him on the wrist and let him off. It actually became a game to Julian.

The last time we went to court, it was because he was fifteen and he had stolen someone's car. By this time he had been in several group homes, we had gone to famiy counselling and we were still at square one. The judge knew him from his prior offences, and Mom and I were nervous because we thought he was really going to get it this time. Julian was laughing in the courtroom, looking as cool as he could be. But this slap on the wrist was the one that broke the straw on the camel's back, so to speak. Mom was finished trying to talk to him and trying to help him adjust. You could see in her eyes that she had lost this battle and was accepting her defeat. They released him back into our custody for a day-visit and then we were supposed to drop him back to the group home where he was staying. Julian bounced out of that courthouse, and by the time we all got on the train to head home, he turned to us and said, "I'll see y'all later. I got business to attend to."

Mom didn't even flinch or say bye. It was over for her. A Children's Aid social worker came to our house that afternoon. She was explaining their position to us and how they could help. Julian had been in seven different group homes and beat up everyone that crossed him the wrong way. The social worker felt that Mom should think about getting him diagnosed and perhaps on some medication. Mom heard what she had to say, but she wasn't listening. She thanked her for coming and giving her the information, but she was not going to make any more decisions for Julian, he would be making them for himself.

As the social worker left, she put her business card on the table. "Well, if you change your mind or need any additional information, please don't hesitate to call."

The day I heard Mom say she wanted no more

police coming to the door was the day Officer Brown came to inform her of Julian's arrest. He had been arrested for assault with a deadly weapon and for theft over $10,000. Julian had tried to steal a yacht. Officer Brown had become acquainted with us through the many encounters with Julian and felt he should come by this time and let Mom know what was going to happen. "Jocelyn, this time the Children's Aid Society is going to ask you if you want to sign him over as a 'ward of the court.' This just means you don't have to come to court any more, deal with police coming to the door, or with Julian. The CAS would take full responsibility for him. Think about it. This is a big charge, and he ain't getting no hand slap on the wrist for this one." He left some papers on the table, shook her hand, and left.

Throughout their conversation I noticed Mommy was listening very closely to everything he was saying. Almost like she had made her decision and this was her way to seal the deal. After he left, she sat there looking at the papers for quite some time. I just knew she wasn't going to do it. This was his biggest charge, and he was really going to need our support now. We couldn't abandon him now. She took up the pen that was left beside the paper and was going to sign it.

I ran to the kitchen table, screaming "Nooo! What are you doing? You can't just give Julian away, Ma, he's our family…he's my brother!" I started to cry hysterically.

Mom tried to console me by telling me that this was going to help him because they have people, like psychologists, that could help him get better. They could do things for him that she felt she couldn't.

"Maybe he will get the male role modelling that he needs and that will help him, and then he could come back and live with us." I couldn't believe what I was hearing.

How could she? How could she just give my brother away like that? I know he's got issues, but this is a totally different country, and he doesn't know anyone. He'll be all alone in court. No way is this good for us, I don't care how she wants to rationalize it. We aren't perfect, but we are family, aren't we? I was so confused. Confused with my own feelings of defense for him. Confused with why she would want to even think about something like that.

"Please, Mommy, please! I'm begging you, please don't do this to him! Don't do this to our family, please!" I ran to the couch and buried my face in the cushion and cried my eyes out. I felt like someone I loved had died, and I didn't get to say goodbye, *again*.

"Dymond, this is for the best." Mommy tried to convince me.

The next time I saw my brother he was in a juvenile facility somewhere up in Northern Ontario. He looked different. He had changed. He had become institutionalized and hard. He actually hugged me and Darrin, but walked right past Mommy. That was the first time I saw what pain and rejection could do to someone else. I knew pain and rejection hurt me and taught me to harden my heart a little, but I never saw what it looked like in someone else's eyes. I never saw it lock down a heart completely. I decided to show him my heart this time.

"Hey, J, I miss you man. You okay in here?"

"Hey, Dymond. Yeah, I'm good."

My heart went out to him. I knew why he was always misbehaving. I knew why he was angry. Yeah, he broke the law, but he wasn't the only one that deserved punishment.

There would be many other times when my brother would get out of one institution just to go right back into another one. He felt more comfortable in a life of crime and rebellion than one of peace and stability. We were a broken family, a damaged family, and we didn't know how to heal.

Julian terrorized my life, always kept me in a state of defense and fear. He beat me more times than I can remember, but he was still my brother and the only other family I had aside from Darrin and Mom. If she could just give up on him like that, it was just a matter of time before she gave up on me. I realized that even though we were in a different country and Mom had changed the way she lived her life, things hadn't changed much. I was on my own in the BX, and I was on my own again here in the Jungle.

We would be separated from Julian for many years before being reunited again, and those moments of reunion were short lived and always filled with hurt and arguments. I had no idea of the life that Julian was going to have without us, but I always looked for him and tried to call him and keep in touch. Mom couldn't think about being his mother anymore. She felt that she had failed him and had no clue what to do. Darrin would ask me for Julian sometimes, and I would tell him he's living with a new family and just leave it at that.

As for me, this was my first heartbreak. I felt scared, lost, and in pieces, but I learned quickly how to mask that pain and how to cope. A bigger part of my heart became cold; it fit with the cold world I lived in, where survival of the fittest was the most important. I felt like I was going to be okay as long as I kept my cold edge and stayed ready for the unexpected. I had no idea there was a bigger heartache coming that would make this pain feel like a soft pinch on the cheek. It would be the pain that would violently slap me across my face and change my life forever.

◈ ◈ ◈

My adolescent years were rocky, confusing, and full of crazy life lessons. I experienced a lot of hardship and heartache before I learned those lessons. Partly because I was so stubborn and angry, and partly because of that defensive wall I had built, brick by brick, that no one could get through.

By the age of twelve, I was fully developed and had 'brothas' in college trying to get my attention. I wasn't interested, but I liked the attention and most times didn't know how to respond to it, so I played it off like I was used to it. Instead of getting involved with boys, I decided to try to get a job. I looked older than I was so I used it to my advantage. I started to work and save my own money. Mom had no idea what I was doing, and I was going to make sure it stayed that way. I wanted to make sure I could take care of myself, just in case Mom wanted to give me away to a group home, too. I wasn't going out like Julian did.

By the time I had turned seventeen, I had lost my best friend Tat, my school, Miss Burnell, Popi, Rafael, and Julian. I had moved to a foreign country that broke up my dysfunctional family to make it more dysfunctional. I started working before I stepped foot into high school. We were still struggling in the hood and living off the government because that's what my mother had been accustomed to, but I was handling my business. I was working and buying groceries, paying my own bills, buying my own clothes and whatever else I needed. Mom lived vicariously through soap operas and night-time television. She was afraid of going out and getting caught up with the street life again, so she threw herself into church.

When I graduated from high school, Mom looked at the diploma and said, "That's nice." That was her way of saying "Congratulations." I don't think she even knew how I was able to pass and graduate. To be honest, I was stumped on that one as well. It was nothing short of a miracle that had me pass all my classes, because I surely didn't apply myself the way I should have. After graduation, I had no clue of who I was supposed to be or what I was supposed to do. I had gone through my adolescent years totally confused, tricking everyone into believing that I had it together. Convincing everyone that I knew exactly what I wanted to do with my life, but I really didn't have any direction. By that time my heart was not just partially hardened, it was fortified and completely walled up. Brick by brick, I had built a very strong wall that wasn't coming down anytime soon.

I never saw myself as beautiful. As a child in the streets of New York, people would stop my mother and say, "What a beautiful baby," and think she was the nanny. I used to look at myself in the mirror for hours to try and see something beautiful and found nothing. Sometimes I would ask her, "Ma, am I beautiful?"

She would always say, "It's more important to be beautiful on the inside than on the outside." Then she'd walk away like she was about to do something. I took that as, "No, you're ugly so stop asking me."

Growing up in Toronto was confusing. I was told my beauty was a blessing and a curse, both at the same time. I used to get mad because I didn't know how that could be. I was still searching for the beauty in myself and couldn't find it. Everything about me was confusing. I was a Black Boricua with tiger eyes, confusing. The colour of my eyes was rare, and it made people trip out. I would constantly hear, "Are those your real eyes?" To make things even more confusing, I had a Coca-cola bottle body shape that came with an ability to play basketball and run track, which got me into way too much trouble. Even my hair was confused. It wasn't exactly curly enough to be an afro because it was too soft to stand up by itself but too thick and wavy to lay down straight. By seventeen, I was going to the hairdresser every two weeks so they could handle it. I tried to learn as much as I could so I could manage it better on my own.

I had grown to love God deeply but hate the church desperately. I found out the hard way that even the mothers of the church could be hypocritical. God was always my Rock. I always believed He heard my prayers. Sometimes He took a long time answering them, but He eventually did with most of them. The ones that didn't get answered I just chalked up to not being meant to be. I had given my heart to God when I was seventeen, believing that He had a plan for my life and that He was going to help me figure it out. With God, I felt a love that I had been missing out on, and I knew that He was going to teach me about the beauty that was hiding inside of me that I couldn't see. I was dedicated. I was in church every Sunday morning and night and every Wednesday night Bible study. Then I confided in an older lady. They called her the mother of the church. I told her something that had happened to me, because I needed help getting through it. I told her on a Wednesday and by the Sunday the whole church knew, and the story had been changed to make me look like I should have been crucified on the cross myself. People started talking behind my back and judging me. I couldn't believe it. I was so devastated that I cursed out the church mother and all the leaders in the church. I was beyond tight. I hadn't let anyone in over the wall for years, but I trusted her because she was a Christian. I believed that God would protect me from liars and let me know when hypocrites were around me. Well, He didn't, and I felt betrayed, once again. So I left Him and all of them.

I partied hard that year, still trying to find out what I was supposed to be doing with my life. Who was I supposed to be? Was there beauty in me? And if there was, what did it look like? How the hell was I going to get rid of all this anger that I still had inside? I was still angry at Mom for breaking up our family and acting like she didn't care about Julian anymore. I was angry at Popi for leaving us and lying to my face. I was angry at the fact that no matter what I did, I always felt less than nothing, even though I pretended like I was more than everything. I was lost, and I needed help. I missed God's presence, but I was not going to go back to church around those hyper-Christians. So I partied even harder and cared even less about what anyone said or thought about me.

One day, Mom and her new friend, Nika, were planning a trip to New York City. Since she had invited her to that prayer meeting and Mom had turned her life over to God, Nika was her biggest supporter. They became inseperable and they both loved to shop. I was due for a shopping spree so I was all over that. I came in and threw my arm over Nika's shoulder. "Yes, my sistas, when we leavin'?"

Nika promptly took my hand off her shoulder and said, "You ain't comin', Dymond. We're going for a church convention in Jamaica, Queens."

"A church convention? Ah, man. Well let me come anyway, and y'all can go to your little convention while I shop on Jamaica Avenue. Ha ha ha."

Mommy saw an opportunity to capitalize on. "You really wanna come, Dymond?"

"Come on, Ma, stop playin'. Yeah, I wanna come. My clothes are played out and I need some outfits that will make me look fresh and fly, you know?"

"Okay, you can come, on one condition…you gotta come to church with us on the Sunday."

"Say what now?"

"You heard me. You can shop on Friday and Saturday but when Sunday comes, you're coming to church with us. Deal?"

I thought about it and decided to take her up on it; maybe it wouldn't be that bad. "Hold on, hold on… just one service on Sunday, right?"

"Yep, one service in the morning."

"Okay, I can do dat."

We travelled for eight hours to New York City. Over the years, I had been back many times and it was always weird. The minute we would enter the city and I could hear the traffic, see the people, and smell the sewer, I felt like I was back in a surrounding that I had left just yesterday. Even though it had been years, it always felt like it was just yesterday. The memories and feelings would flood to the surface of my heart, and I would feel a strange sense of belonging. In Toronto, I always felt lost. I felt like no one understood me. In NYC, especially the Bronx, I didn't have to explain myself all the time, they just got me. Plus there were all kinds of young women just like me. Beautiful Black Latinas that were mixed like me and who didn't look at me like I had three heads. I still got compliments on my eyes, but I saw a couple of people with similar eye colour. In short, I always felt at home.

The weekend went great. I shopped and got deals I was sure I would never get in Toronto. I knew I was going to go back looking better than most of the people that I called friends, because they didn't have the same selections that I had to choose from. The church was all the way in Queens, and we were staying in Brooklyn. So we got up early Sunday morning and headed out to the last day of the convention. All weekend, Nika and Mommy were talking about how God was doing this and God was doing that. I pretended like I wasn't listening and it didn't matter to me, but secretly it did. I wanted to feel Him, too. I felt like I needed Him. I just wasn't willing to take down one brick from this wall. The last time I took down a brick it only led to humiliation and hurt.

We got there while the praise and worship team were already singing. I had grown up in church so I knew most of the songs, but there was a different feeling in this church. I sat there for a while without singing, but it was too much for me to hold back. I felt the melody coming from my stomach through my chest, entering my vocal chords, and before I knew it, the melody was coming out of my mouth, and my hand was starting to go up. I quickly caught it and left the sanctuary, pretending to go to the bathroom. I almost ran to the door. Once outside the sanctuary door, I closed my eyes since I was by myself. I could still hear the music and the congregation singing, and I wanted to sing to the Lord from my heart without the expectation or pressure of getting saved. So I sang out by myself,

"Without a doubt we know that we have been revived, when we shall leave this place. Sweet Holy Spirit. Sweet Heavenly Dove. Stay right here with us, filling us with your love…"

Before I knew it, my hands were up, my eyes were closed, and I was singing from my heart to the One who loved me best. I missed Him, and I wanted to know if I could have Him without the hassle of the church. I felt torn but compelled to continue singing full out. No one was around so I didn't feel constricted at all. Just then, I heard a voice come from behind me.

"Hey, nice voice."

Who? What? Where did he come from?

Kevaughn was 6' 3" with soft eyes and the most genuine smile. He looked like he was as young as me, but what was he doing in church ushering? You could tell he played basketball because he had that basketball walk, like he was used to carrying a heavy gym bag. Yeah, he had that walk, but it looked cool on him. I imagined his physique under the suit looked like he was athletic. His skin was caramel. I was startled and confused at the same time but managed to say, "Oh, thank you." It was really weird how he had just appeared there. I didn't hear anyone come into that area at all.

The church service was actually refreshing, and I felt compelled to go to the altar, but I didn't because I didn't want my mother and Nika to put any pressure on me, especially since I had to drive back with them another eight hours. When church was done, we went next door to their bookstore. Kevaughn was there behind the cash register cashing people out. He saw me and decided to come over and talk to me, again.

"How did you like the service today?"

"It's my first time here, but I thought it was really good." We continued to talk about random things— the sermon, the worship, some of the books, me living in Canada, and on and on. The whole time we spoke, I felt the craziest thing. I just knew that I knew him and we had met before. I started to ask him where he lived and we found out that we both were from the Bronx. I thought maybe we knew each other as kids, but that wasn't it. It was something else. I just couldn't put my finger on it. We walked outside and decided to write each other and keep in touch. He had never been to Canada and wanted to come and see it one day. He was cool, my age, loved God, and was pretty dedicated to church.

Nika and Mommy were ready to go and were giving me the look. Before I said goodbye I had to ask him one very important question. "Hey, listen, Kevaughn, I know we just met but I have to ask you this."

"Yeah, sure. Shoot."

"How is it that you can be young like me and deal

with the hypocrites in church?"

He chuckled, and his smile did something to my heart that I wasn't expecting. It took a brick down and weakened my wall. "Ah, man, they got hypocrites everywhere—church, work, school, in the hood…you just gotta keep your eyes focused on Christ. It's about Him not them."

That made sense theoretically, but I didn't know how to live that out. I wished we had more time to talk so he could break that down for me. We shook hands and promised to keep in touch. I actually believed he wanted to, and something inside me felt compelled to keep in touch with him, too. As I walked toward the car, I couldn't help feeling like that conversation was just one of many we had already. I felt like my heart knew him, even though I was just meeting him for the first time. My soul knew him and knew it would be okay for me to trust him, but my mind and heart were bugging out. My heart was racing and screaming in my head. *Girl, you betta pick that brick up and place it back on the wall to protect yourself!* But I didn't. I couldn't. The safety and comfort that I felt talking to him was something I had never experienced before. It didn't feel like I was going to have to get to know a stranger; it felt more like there were moments that we had encountered before, and conversation with him just brought back those memories. I was so grateful for that small conversation. This was one of the first times in my life that I was aware of a soulful connection, and I felt the hand of God reach through his heart to mine.

My life was changing, and even though I had just met Kevaughn, a brick was taken from my wall, and I should have felt defenseless, but I didn't. I felt safe and right and beautiful. I had been talking to Kevaughn, but my heart was engaged in an intimate moment with the love of God. I didn't know it then, but I had gotten air breathed into my wings, and I was about to take off and start to fly. All because of *him*.

Look, I'm Flying!

"With the right amount of oxygen in a butterfly's wings it will fly and soar to places it had only dreamed of before. Beautiful and free. Until it's time to die and be born again." ~Dymond

I got back to Toronto and knew that life would never be the same. I didn't know how exactly, but I knew things were going to change, drastically. Every day I expected God to do something. I didn't know what was going to happen, but I had a new expectation of Him. I wanted to experience His presence more, and I felt Him drawing me. I felt in my heart He was saying, "Come close."

Kevaughn and I actually wrote to each other. It was funny how even through his letters I understood him and felt like he understood me in a way that most didn't get. We were becoming good friends. We decided to use the phone to keep in touch. We spoke for hours about all kinds of stuff. He was so easy to talk to and would always answer my questions about God and being a Christian as a young man. I never had a cross-country friend before, yet he was becoming my closest friend. Little by little, my bricks were coming down and I was learning how to let someone in. I was a bit nervous, but every time I received a letter or we spoke, all the unknown stuff that would freak me out became known. I couldn't put a name to it, but I just knew him and that was enough for me.

I had decided to go to college and figure it out step by step, bit by bit. I felt like I was getting a second chance at life. Where there was a feeling of loss, I felt like now I had found something special. The shock was that that something special was in *me*. The whole time. I felt God calling my name, even though I had turned my back on Him. And one night, after speaking to Kevaughn on the phone, in my bedroom, I decided to surrender one more time. This time there was no huge altar call, no prayer workers ready to lay hands on me with anointing oil, no music in the background to manipulate my emotions. It was just me and Him. It was quiet, aside from my sniffling because of the tears that came without warning. I couldn't go another day just thinking about God; I needed Him. I needed His love, His grace, His understanding, His music that He always put in my heart.

I needed His healing.

I needed Him.

I asked Him to give me another chance as I felt His Holy Spirit flood my room. I was filled with love. His presence was so real. I couldn't speak words in English. But He understood me. I felt Him receive my apology and forgive me. I felt brand new. My heart's wall had been seriously damaged and now was under new construction.

I was free. Free to fly and be exactly what God wanted me to be. I didn't know what that was exactly, but I knew that He knew, and I trusted Him to lead me to it.

Life had changed for me, and there was peace and joy that I couldn't understand completely, but I also couldn't stop talking about it to everyone I knew. I felt like nothing could get me down. I had a new lease on life, and I wasn't going to let anyone mess with it. Not the hypocrites, not Mommy, not Darrin, not the little boys that pretended to be men just to get into my pants, no one.

My life had changed, and I was on the right path. I had no idea that this joy, this love, was going to lead me right to my destiny, where I would experience the deepest pain I had ever had in my life. All the other pains and hardships would take a backseat to this tragedy. It would violently slap me across the face and change the course of my life, forever. I would be forced to choose to change again. My dreams would be shattered in a way that I had never before experienced or imagined. It didn't matter if I was ready or not, it was going to happen.

So the metamorphosis continues…

A Dymond Story